THE
FERGUSON
EFFECT

Also by Harry Harris from Orion

Ruud Gullit: The Chelsea Diary

THE FERGUSON EFFECT

Harry Harris

ORION

The right of Harry Harris to be identified as the author of this
work has been asserted by him in accordance with the
Copyright, Designs and Patents Act 1988

First published in Great Britain in 1999 by
Orion Media
An imprint of Orion Books Ltd
Orion House, 5 Upper St Martin's Lane, London WC2H 9EA

A CIP catalogue record for this book is available
from the British Library

ISBN 0 75281 794 9

Filmset by Selwood Systems, Midsomer Norton
Printed and bound by
Butler & Tanner Ltd, Frome and London

CONTENTS

ACKNOWLEDGEMENTS

Special thanks to Roddy Forsyth of the *Daily Telegraph* for his expert insight into Alex Ferguson and for specialising in his life and times north of the border. Dennis Signy of the Football Writers' Association also made a valuable contribution together with the *Mirror*'s Manchester correspondent, Steve Miller. I would also like to thank lifelong United fans Colin Gibson, sports editor of the *Sunday Telegraph*, and Steve Curry, also of the *Sunday Telegraph*, for their contributions and advice, together with Neil Harman of the same newspaper. Orion editor Simon Spanton deserves recognition for devising the format which has created a perceptive insight into the personal life and career of one of soccer's most significant figures this century.

FOREWORD

By the Right Honourable Tony Banks, Minister of Sport

The day I hear the chant of 'Stand up if you hate Chelsea' is the day I know my club will have cracked it. In football, as in politics, jealousy is a rampant force. It stops people analysing objectively why they are failing whilst others succeed. Alex Ferguson has become one of football's most successful managers ever and he certainly takes some stick for it. Of course, Manchester United were a world-renowned club when he took over but such legacies usually make it more rather than less difficult to succeed. Expectation runs at absurdly high levels and fans are impatient. It was a tribute to Alex's vision and the United board's faith that when things were really difficult at the beginning both sides stuck it out. The subsequent rewards proved just how right both were.

Manchester United have become the premier league club against which all others judge themselves, and the great majority are found wanting. Never slow to enter the transfer market at the top end, Alex Ferguson has also been astute enough to continue developing the club's youth policy. As a result United are now the mainstay of the England team, and both sides rely on Alex's ability to continue breeding success.

As you may guess, I think Alex Ferguson is the best but my admiration for his management skills is equalled by my respect for his politics. In a game where greed and selfishness are commonplace Alex has remained true to his roots. Success has doubtless brought him wealth and great fame but he has spurned the flashiness adopted by some of his contemporaries which can turn the heads of young players and ruin them both on and off the pitch. No wonder the young players at United have been able to fulfil their true soccer potential. They have had a great role model.

Alex Ferguson will no doubt go on to more footballing triumphs, and when the fans are standing up, claiming to hate Man United, ironically they are paying Alex and his club their greatest tribute.

PREFACE

There are few people who know The Real Alex Ferguson.

Those who do have contributed to this unique insight into the secrets of Ferguson's life and career. Ferguson's friends, colleagues, associates, those who have played for him and worked for him at both Aberdeen and Manchester United. The chairmen, the agents, the game's administrators. Even the dreaded media – written press, radio and TV personalities.

Friend and foe alike have a common bond of admiration for Ferguson's success. Together they paint a portrait of what makes Fergie tick ... The Ferguson Effect. It's a virtual *Who's Who* of football. Anyone who is anyone in the game has been more than willing to provide thoughts, views and anecdotes about a living legend in management.

And some surprises are unearthed. For example, both Spurs and Arsenal approached Ferguson to become their manager. Arsenal opted for George Graham instead, while Tottenham actually offered Ferguson the post and he accepted! Irving Scholar shook hands with Ferguson on the deal and only a last-minute change of heart prevented the course of soccer history being altered – Ferguson becoming boss at White Hart Lane to succeed Keith Burkinshaw.

While Graham proved to be the right choice for Highbury, until he was unseated by bung allegations, Scholar was convinced that Ferguson would have revitalised the other end of north London. Maybe all that success Ferguson has brought to Old Trafford was destined for Spurs.

And for the first time former Football Association chief executive Graham Kelly reveals just how close England came to appointing the first Scotsman to manage their national side.

These are just some of the insights into the life and times of Ferguson through the eyes of the people he has encountered throughout his fascinating and highly successful career – a more comprehensive insight than even Ferguson might provide himself!

Fittingly this in-depth study comes at a time when he still has plenty to prove.

Ferguson's mission is to regain Manchester United's domination of the domestic game surrendered to Arsenal, but of paramount importance is to win the elusive Champions' League.

Ferguson paid tribute to the achievements of Arsenal and Arsene Wenger, the Frenchman who became the first foreign coach to win the elusive Double.

The game had changed for ever, with Ruud Gullit starting the silverware revolution of the foreign coaches at the Bridge and Luca Vialli landing a double of his own as an English team – well, French, Italian, et al – brought home a European trophy.

London Pride. The southern softies ending northern domination. Ferguson had something to say about that. Ferguson broke Kevin Keegan's will in the battle with Newcastle, but his mind games didn't work with Wenger. He met his match there.

Those who consider Ferguson to be a moaning whinger who rarely gives credit where credit is due, would have been shocked when the deposed boss of the champions was in effusive mood about Arsenal's Double.

He said: 'Arsene Wenger deserved success. It was very important to him to win. He's had some criticism and so have I but to come through and win something makes it all worthwhile. Winning the Double is very important – very few teams have done it. When you look at 120 years of football and see how few teams have done it, it shows just what an achievement it is. It isn't the highlight of my career, though. That was winning the Premiership for the first time because I had achieved what I set out to. Arsenal did exceptionally well to win the league. We were only one point behind so we hope that perhaps next season we can win the league by a point.

'All the young United players have the temperament and the ability to do well. You can't stop progress and you can't stop young people with great potential playing. If you're good enough you're old enough.

'Getting into the Champions' League was really important to us. We've had a degree of success. We were disappointed not to get beyond

Monaco last season but injuries took their toll. We were desperately unlucky against Borussia Dortmund the year before. Hopefully it will be third time lucky. The players will get better each time they play.'

The bookies believed this was going to be Ferguson's final season as manager of Manchester United. At the start of the season they made horse-owning Fergie a near-rails runner at 5–2 not to be in control by the summer. William Hill believed he would move 'upstairs' and guide the club with the same love and affection as Sir Matt Busby.

They issued their annual odds on managers 'no longer to be in their current job by the end of the season'. Evens: Alan Curbishley; Christian Gross. 6–4: Jim Smith; Joe Kinnear. 7–4: Kenny Dalglish; Dave Bassett; Martin O'Neill. 2–1: Gordon Strachan. 5–2: Alex Ferguson; Bryan Robson; Dave Jones. 3–1: Gianluca Vialli, Harry Redknapp. 4–1: Arsene Wenger; Roy Hodgson; John Gregory. 6–1: Danny Wilson. 8–1: George Graham; Walter Smith. 10–1: Gerard Houllier.

Dalglish and Gross fell at the second fence, Roy Evans, Dave Bassett and Roy Hodgson didn't make it, but the evergreen 'Fergie' was negotiating a *three year* extension to his existing contract. Ferguson's unquenchable ambition was matched by the club's £28m worth of signings – Dwight Yorke, Jaap Stam and Jesper Blomqvist.

And his influence will live on. A number of his players at Aberdeen moved into management, influenced by him, as has Steve Bruce, the inspiration and soul of Manchester United's first three Premiership titles under Ferguson.

Elevated from Birmingham City's playing staff, Ferguson's references for his former captain rely heavily on metaphors of human spirit. 'If any footballer has made himself into a top-class performer on a heart the size of a dustbin lid, it's this man,' Ferguson said.

Bruce is flattered. 'I was never naturally gifted, but I wanted to play in the top division and I did it by hard work and effort.' Of all Ferguson's management virtues, Bruce most wants to emulate a driven, insatiable need to win. 'I hope I've learned from Fergie. He is very, very clever. His attention to detail is fantastic. He's learned from other countries. Brian Kidd was all over Europe five or six years ago, watching different coaching methods and introducing detailed diets. But the one thing I hope I've learned most from Fergie is his unbelievable desire to win, and I think the way you get that across to players is in the way you handle situations, the way people look at you.'

INTRODUCTION

Alex Ferguson, OBE and CBE, is arguably the greatest British manager of modern times. Awarded the OBE after Aberdeen's European Cup Winners' Cup win over Real Madrid, he received the CBE in the 1995 New Year's Honours List for his formidable achievements at Manchester United. He ended United's 26-year wait for the championship when he delivered the title to Old Trafford in 1993.

The overriding assessment is that Ferguson deserves to be considered alongside the icons of football management of all time – Shankly, Sir Matt Busby, Stein and Paisley.

The achievement of 15 major trophies in English football speaks for itself with pressure of more to come this season. Fergie's haul includes four Premiership crowns, three FA Cups, the European Cup Winners' Cup, League Cup, European Super Cup and five Charity Shields' – a magnificent return for 12 years' reign at Old Trafford.

In addition, he was one of the most successful bosses north of the border, with nine trophies at Pittodrie where he steered Aberdeen to three Premier League titles and four Scottish Cup triumphs, plus the League Cup and the European Cup Winners' Cup. A total of *twenty-four trophies*.

Ferguson moved to Old Trafford in November 1986 and took the Red Devils to an FA Cup Final replay victory over Crystal Palace in 1990 to become the first man to manage cup-winning clubs north and south of the border. Just a year later he regained Manchester United's reputation abroad with the European Cup Winners' Cup triumph, then in 1992 the League Cup went to Old Trafford for the first time and in 1993 his United team won the inaugural Premier League. A year on Ferguson guided United to the FA Cup and Premiership Double. He followed that with the League and FA Cup Double in 1996 – the Double Double. Following Jock Stein's untimely and tragic death, he took charge of Scotland's team in the 1986 World Cup Finals.

Ferguson cannot yet envisage a life without football, but he might have to consider a life outside the firing line at Old Trafford one day.

He dismisses speculation of his retirement. He showed with his passion in one of his typical pitch-side bust-ups at Ewood Park last season what the game still means to him. The emotion keeps him young, gives him the zest, the hunger to carry on as he refuses to let age weary him.

'Everyone says: "When are you going to retire, Alex?" And I reply: "What the hell am I going to do if I do pack it in?" I've bought racehorses but I would soon get bored of them, don't worry. Besides, I don't think anyone likes change. The players have grown up here and they know who the manager is every day. They know I have always looked after them. I am sure they would rather have me than not. I would miss all the aggro as well. What would I do with myself? Speculation about when I might retire quite frankly bugs me. I'm fed up with people trying to pigeonhole me for retirement. I feel as fit as I ever did and have a lot more to achieve. I intend to work into my sixties because Manchester United are my life.'

He intends to continue until he can deliver the last of the historic collection, the European Cup, one day returning it to its 1968 home.

Alex Ferguson is a Jekyll and Hyde character – sometimes charming, sometimes confrontational. The mood swings are amazing; they are also legendary – from a smiling, approachable, warm individual to a man capable of a torrent of abuse and vitriol. Personally, I have witnessed both sides of his character and there's no prize for guessing which one I prefer!

But there is no questioning his pedigree as a manager. There is no harder worker in the game, attending public functions, arranging meetings and overseeing training.

His roots no doubt dictate the work ethic. Alex began his career representing Govan High School, Glasgow Schools and Scotland Schools before joining Queens Park FC, Glasgow, as an amateur in 1957.

The teenage Ferguson, an apprentice toolmaker, organised an illegal strike because he thought management was about to cut wages. He went on to play for Rangers and St Johnstone.

He served his managerial apprenticeship at lowly East Stirling and then St Mirren. The St Mirren spell turned sour and he was sacked. He sued the club for wrongful dismissal but lost at a damaging industrial tribunal. He learned his managerial trade at Aberdeen, reeling off league titles, trophies and the European Cup Winners' Cup and Super Cup.

Success really came as a manager rather than a player, first at Aberdeen. Then came his amazing success at Manchester United. Ferguson's domain is his office at the Cliff. On the cabinet, next to the bookshelves crammed with yearbooks and Manchester United programme collections, there are a couple of framed photographs: Ferguson with Jack Charlton; Ferguson with Bob Paisley. Letters and faxes and football magazines compete for space on his desk. To his right, a sign is pinned on the wall, where it cannot be missed, a bald tribute to his Glasgow heritage. It is printed in capital letters and it says: 'HACUMFIGOVAN.'

A normal day at the office starts with a 6 a.m. alarm call at home. Fergie rises in the plush stockbroker belt of Cheshire. By 7.30 a.m. he is off in his luxury car and heading along the 15-mile route to United's Cliff training ground, arriving around 8.15 a.m. Some mornings he's driving through the gates at 7.45 a.m.

He enjoys a simple bowl of cereal and studies the back pages of the newspapers that lie on the table next to the slices of melon and the pieces of toast. After a cuppa, the first of many phone calls are made and received from his office high above the practice pitch. He will have a workout and shower before the players arrive at 9.45 a.m. He goes through the same routine even if he is feeling unwell.

Ferguson is locked in discussions with coaching staff preparing for 10 a.m. when training begins, with Ferguson's assistant putting United's stars through routines devised by former assistant Brian Kidd after coaching trips to Italy. At 10.30 a.m. Fergie joins new assistant Steve McClaren on the pitch when the main work of the day is in full flow. At 12.15 p.m. Fergie will shower and change before meeting the media – radio first, followed by the press. At 1 p.m. it's time for a light lunch and a drive across the city to Old Trafford for an afternoon of meetings, arriving back home at around 4 p.m. to freshen up before heading off anywhere in the country to take in a game. Most evenings his day ends at 11 p.m.

This is in stark contrast to the working schedule of the in-vogue player–managers. Ruud Gullit was sacked for a myriad of reasons, the truth still being hard to fathom out, but points enigmatic chairman Ken Bates made were the Dutchman's lack of work ethic and his time-consuming commercial deals which deflected his attention. Yet Bates appointed Gullit stressing that he didn't expect him to be driving up and down the motorway looking at reserve-team players at Northampton.

Recognition of Gullit's achievements was not slow in coming from one of his principal rivals. Ferguson believed that Gullit posed as much, if not more, of a threat as Arsene Wenger at Highbury. Having acknowledged that he was shocked by Gullit's sacking, Ferguson went on to praise him as a healthy presence in English football:

'I have always found him relaxed and easy to get on with – a good winner and a good loser. He said a few outrageous things in terms of management but he was refreshing and I think he was good for the game. Ruud tried to play the continental way in this country and that requires a delicate touch to operate it successfully.

'He overplayed his hand at times with varying selections but he was trying to maintain a challenge on every front by keeping a sharp edge to his squad. You could see the reasoning behind the frequent rotation of his strikers. He didn't make as many changes in other positions. Gianluca Vialli and Mark Hughes are well into their thirties and he obviously thought they would be fresher if he didn't play them all the time. But big players have big egos and there were bound to be problems.'

There was, of course, one important contrast between Gullit and Ferguson. At the time of Gullit's sacking the pizza commercials had a high profile on TV. Meanwhile, on Friday evening Ferguson was busy checking on Monaco, United's next opponents in the European Cup, then he took a Saturday-morning plane from Nice to Munich so that he could catch a connecting flight for Birmingham, where he watched Aston Villa as part of his homework for the Premier League meeting at Villa Park. With a home FA Cup tie against Barnsley, that gave him a schedule of attending three widely scattered matches in less than 48 hours.

It is difficult to imagine the highly social Dutchman displaying enthusiasm for such a programme. Gullit re-emerged in the British game, replacing Kenny Dalglish at St James' after only the second game of the season (ironically a 1–1 draw at Chelsea) and despite still awaiting his first signing (Darren Ferguson) pulled off a 0–0 draw at Old Trafford.

Whatever the contrast in philosophies, the two have immense mutual respect for each other, and Ferguson invited Gullit to join him at the Cliff training ground whenever he was free to do so, prior to his appointment at Newcastle United.

There cannot be a Premiership manager who works harder than Ferguson. Nor can there be one with more genuine passion for the game.

Oliver Holt of *The Times* interviewed Ferguson in his training-ground office not long before the end of a depressing season when it was certain that his team would end up potless. 'You see all these books, bloody magazines, odd bits of chewing gum, videos, everything, training things, all this wine, boots, umbrellas, everything,' he told Holt. 'That's great, but it also tells you about the baggage you collect as a manager here. There's always somebody that wants some part of you and that's the exhausting bit.

'As a younger man, I was always with the players. In the afternoons I was always here. Now I'm here or at Old Trafford and I'm bouncing between the bloody two of them all the time. So, thereby, you lose the love of the real thing and the other part comes into it. You have to be mentally tuned in to all the things you are going to have to do in the day. My diary is horrendous.

'It's that kind of thing that makes you say to yourself: "I could do without this." But then you ask yourself, "Well, what would you do if you retired, if you didn't have United – what would you do then?" That is a more distressing outlook. That is distressing to think about, particularly when you know you are only 56.

'What I have got to do is find a new way of surviving. It may be done by changing the team, by giving myself new targets; it may be done by redefining my job in a couple of years' time. But, whatever, I will have to find a way of surviving and also being here so that really is the answer to you. It is difficult to think you are going to quit.

'I've had a lot of offers. You get offers all the time and some of them are very interesting offers about taking over clubs and things like that, but would they give me the satisfaction of Man United? You do not want to let it go.'

One such offer came from Inter Milan three years ago but Ferguson opted to stay at Old Trafford to fulfil his destiny – to emulate the Old Trafford legend that is Sir Matt Busby, and to do that he must deliver the European Cup.

Ferguson might have wanted Ronaldo and even bid for Gabriel Batistuta and Patrick Kluivert, but he eventually paid a club record of £12.6 million for Dwight Yorke.

Fergie said: 'Front players nowadays need courage and stamina – there are a lot of demands on them. Dwight's laid-back facade helps him cope with those demands. He is always smiling but there is a wee bit of spark in him. The best example of that type of temperament is Ronaldo. He gets kicked all the time but he keeps his cool, keeps going and plays great football. In a different sort of way, Dwight has got that kind of temperament.'

The signing of Yorke, 26, took United's spending to £28 million. But Ferguson revealed he would have been willing to take his spree towards the £40 million mark if the bid for Patrick Kluivert had not collapsed. He went on: 'When we decided we needed a striker, Dwight was the first one we went for. The Kluivert situation came about because Milan let us know that he was available. But we would still have bought Dwight even if we had got Kluivert. We have always known about Dwight's ability. He has played in different positions – wide on the right and wide on the left. But we have always seen him as an out-and-out striker. Twenty-six is a good age to get a striker and, hopefully, we will get the best five years of his career.'

The summer spree began with the signing of Jaap Stam for a world record fee for a defender – £10.75 million. Together with his salary and signing-on fee and a seven-year contract, the total investment in his first signing after the title went to Arsenal is an astonishing £22 million.

'I do not think the club has peaked at all,' he said. 'I think the potential of the club is never-ending. I think that it's still a new club, really. The club has got to get to grips with what actually makes a winning club in Europe. It has not approached that. It is not even anywhere near that. It is not a Barcelona, it is not an AC Milan, it is not a Juventus, it's not a Real Madrid. In terms of the quality of the club, it is. In terms of the people working in it and the effort the players put in, it is. But other clubs have a mentality that is different from our mentality. What may happen after I leave is that it will dawn on them that when a new manager comes in he may ask for £60 million to build a team to win in Europe.

'But they may not get the best manager to replace me. And then the dawning part comes in and they will say, "I wish we had done that five years back down the road." There are big strides this club has got to take, but when they will do it, I don't know.'

Chairman Martin Edwards established that the funds were available to Ferguson, and that there were no barriers erected by the board. Having already invested heavily in Jaap Stam, there was £50 million pledged to restore United's power base with massive team rebuilding. Edwards said: 'This is the time on the football calendar for us to kick in with some more heavy investments. You might say we have had it cushy recently after seven or eight years winning a lot of trophies at Old Trafford.

'Now Arsenal have caught us up and it's time for us to act upon that situation. We had to decide whether the framework of this squad needed strengthening again to go and win the Premiership title next season along with success in Europe.

'We have brought in Jaap Stam for some fairly hefty money but we are still looking at other areas. There is more money available and we want to go for an extra midfield player and a striker. If we can find the right men, of course. We have a shopping list which we are working our way through. Of course, we could run into the same situation of last summer with deals that fell through. But clearly we will be making efforts to get in top-quality players. We know this is the time to strengthen because we were so disappointed to go out of the Champions' League. That proved our squad needed deepening.

'But there was also a feeling towards the end of last season that both Arsenal and Liverpool could have won the title with a strong run. This season Arsenal have done that and they have overtaken us. So I think that in the last two years there has definitely been a catching-up process. There used to be a gap and we were reasonably comfortable. Now that gap has been closed. What we are now trying to do is to address that situation again and re-open the gap.'

Ferguson wanted midfield hard man Marc-Vivien Foé, but it broke down after the clubs disagreed over a £2.5 million asking price. Ferguson watched the Lens giant in the French Cup Final defeat by Paris St Germain. The Cameroon international also received approaches from AC Milan and Marseille.

Martin Edwards feels some clubs may be trying to cash in on the club's wealth when haggling over players. United's initial attempts to sign Marc-Vivien Foé failed after the French club hiked up their asking price. United made an improved offer, believed to be worth £5 million, but that was still not enough for Lens who wanted £8 million for the 23-year-old defensive midfielder. Before signing Stam, Edwards suggested the club would not become involved in 'a Dutch auction', but they still ended up paying PSV Eindhoven a world record fee for a defender.

Edwards stressed United are not the only big club which selling sides feel they can take advantage of. 'I don't want to be critical of other clubs, but clearly I would say when the bigger clubs come in for a player the selling club knows they can perhaps offer more than the others,' he said. 'That's a fact of life and we've known about that for a while.'

He said there was little they could do in cases where the player was under contract because the selling club would always hold the upper hand in transfer negotiations, but he would not let anyone hold United to ransom. 'If a player is under contract then obviously the club are free to set the price,' he said. 'The club will be looking at what it will cost them to replace the player if they do sell him. With Stam there were other people around who were prepared to pay that price. It's a question of valuation and how far you are prepared to go. When we look at a player we assess his value and we're not prepared to go beyond that.'

But the really big prize would be the purchase of Gabriel Batistuta, and it's a measure of Ferguson's ambition that he vigorously pursued the Argentinian super-striker even though he was valued at £12 million. But Fiorentina's president, Vittorio Cecchi Gori, presented the new coach of the team, veteran Giovanni Trapattoni, and said 'once again and for ever' that the Argentinian striker is not on sale. 'Gabriel has a rich contract with Fiorentina through 2000. He has never been on sale,' said Cecchi Gori, a movie-industry tycoon and politician.

Trapattoni, who joined Fiorentina for the next season, leaving Bayern Munich, said that Fiorentina needed to keep Batistuta to go for the league title. Batistuta, who has starred with Fiorentina since 1991, said in interviews he wanted to move to get new motivation. The 29-year-old striker, who led Argentina's offensive in the World Cup, was also sought by such big clubs as Roma, Lazio and Parma.

Edwards and Ferguson were busy in their own back yard as well as abroad, with Paul Scholes and Nicky Butt agreeing new seven-year deals to join Gary and Phil Neville on similar £1 million-a-year contracts until 2005. Ole Gunnar Solskjaer has a six-year deal and Ryan Giggs, Andy Cole and Ronny Johnsen five-year deals. David Beckham was involved in talks extending his contract, too, until 2005.

Edwards firmly believes that these gold securities and future spending plans finally nail stories that the former English champions lack investment ambition. He adds: 'I don't think we have ever shown that to be the case. Much of the criticism of us has been made with ignorance. We made three £10 million bids last summer which were unsuccessful because the clubs in question wouldn't release the players.'

However, even England defender Gary Neville didn't feel safe with the expectation of big changes in playing personnel. He said: 'I have seen better players than Gary Neville being sold, I have seen better players than Gary Neville being dropped and I can't afford to think that the manager is not going to drop or sell me. There is already a new defender here and you have to think that with the defenders we have got it is going to be even more difficult to get into the team next season. You can't afford to take your foot off the gas and relax.'

The re-signing of Giggs has been viewed as vital to the continued momentum of the team. Gary Neville observed: 'Ryan feels he can obviously win a lot of things here. And that's important for the young players who want to remain at Old Trafford. They like winning. Once you get that habit you don't want to lose it. That's encouraging. Ryan would be wanted by any club in the world, or at least those who could afford him. So it's great that he has signed. That part of the club is OK.

'It's the same for the other players. Any of them can move these days. You are never safe. But these boys want to be here and we are very lucky in that respect. It's a good club – there's no question about that. Most people want to play for us. The young players are looked after well and we are now reaping the reward for that.'

The Welsh international's injury problems might just have scuppered the annual Old Trafford championship charge. But Giggs insisted the title would only be on loan to north London. 'When we failed to beat West Ham on the last day of the 94/95 season and Blackburn won the title, it made us even more determined. It's not as disastrous as some people make out. No one is ever going to win the League year after year. The Premiership has become so competitive. Every year the chasing teams become stronger and you can't legislate for slip-ups and injuries no matter how big a club you are.

'We still feel we are the best. And in some respects, missing out will probably make us stronger. When we missed out in 1995, we stepped up a gear the next season. We learnt from our mistakes and we became tougher, more resilient. You have to be honest – Arsenal have done well. They went through a bad spell at Christmas and then came through that to stake their claim for the title. Their form has been very consistent, and you need that to win the title. But obviously we are very disappointed with our form. We let them through the back door. When someone is challenging you as strongly as they are, you need to be winning your games. We've dropped points when we should have won games, particularly at home, and they have taken advantage of that.'

Even so, Giggs dismisses claims that United are responsible for their own downfall, undermining their title challenge to concentrate on Europe. 'It was difficult for us in a way because we have had so much success in the Premiership over the past five years. I had always maintained that this team would never be perceived as a great team until European success followed. But to suggest we took the League for granted is not true. Of course we wanted to win the European Cup, but our priority was always both. It's all very well winning the European Cup, but you always want to retain your standing as the best team in England – that goes without saying.

'I mean, there are a lot of people who will be happy if we end up with nothing this season. But that's the challenge you face. Every team, every opposing fan, wants to see you lose. And they do that for a reason. They do it because you are the best team in the country and no matter who you are, if you are successful people want to see you fail. To go out of Europe a few days after losing to Arsenal at Old Trafford was a massive blow for the club. I don't think anyone welcomed the break from Europe after qualifying. We were on top of our game and the way we were playing we felt we could beat anyone. In the end injuries probably beat us. At full strength we would have gone through to the semi-finals.

'I don't know any player who likes to be injured. When things are not going well, you're always thinking to yourself, "If only I could play." I felt at times during this season that I have played the best football of my career. I've been very pleased with my form. But I've struggled with injuries. I probably missed the most critical games of the season.'

It was to be a busy summer of player turnover.

Brian McClair – the loyal Scot once tipped as a possible successor to Ferguson – was freed by Manchester United after eleven years at the club. He was told his contract would not be renewed. It was a major surprise as cult hero McClair, one of Ferguson's best buys from Celtic, was rated a certainty to become a member of staff.

As a long-serving player, who wrote a regular column for the club's magazine, McClair was seen by many as a manager for United in the next century. Interested clubs who enquired about McClair in the past were told he was lined up for a post behind the scenes, but that all ended abruptly. McClair was philosophical when he said: 'I want to keep playing, I feel I've got two good years left in me yet. I was trying to make my mind up about my future, but now that decision has been taken for me. I don't know quite how I feel at the moment. I've enjoyed all of my time at Manchester United but now I will try to find a new club.' The former Scotland international added: 'I don't want to look back in a couple of years and wish I had still been playing. It's time that you just can't get back; it's lost for ever. I'd not been thinking about the coaching side just yet. I would love to carry on at a good level anywhere. Basically I am open to offers.'

McClair, 34, was in the United first team only a few times last season but was mainly used as a trusted captain of the reserves, helping the youngsters come through. Ferguson also relied on the player to assist some of his kids sign new contracts and handle the negotiations on their behalves. The United boss did not let agents near some of his best youngsters and McClair, as a former Scottish PFA chairman like Fergie, was the ideal middle man.

Within the club it was thought inevitable that McClair, one of Ferguson's favourite sons, would be weaned in management with one of the junior sides. The decision to let him go came as a major surprise and appears to have been down to the board rather than the manager.

McClair was one of United's all-time star buys, costing – a tribunal decided – £850,000 in July 1987 when Ferguson pinched him from Celtic as one of his first captures. Ironically McClair still has the League scoring record of 25 goals in a campaign, a total which Andy Cole has been closing in on. Cole took McClair's number nine jersey a couple of years ago but the Scot was happy to stay at the club, claiming that other players never felt the same when they left United.

McClair was rewarded with a testimonial against his old club Celtic and a bumper gate swelled his personal coffers by close to £400,000. The former university student and Labour voter was not looking for a further killing as he planned to prolong his playing days after leaving Manchester United. Ferguson was happy to help out one of his best lieutenants who has played around 350 games for the club, one of the last long-term servants in top-flight football.

Ferguson was also willing to let winger Ben Thornley and centre half Chris Casper leave as he moved out players to bring in new faces. Thornley came in as Ryan Gigg's understudy in the title campaign. The home-grown left winger came back from a career-threatening knee ligament injury, but Ferguson helped him move. Casper, son of former Burnley boss Frank, could have made only a couple of first-team appearances and quit Old Trafford too.

Ferguson was given the mandate from the board to go out there in a blaze of glory. But he is unable to change – still striving, still hungry.

So, how does the man relax?

'My father loved the horses.' Ferguson smiled. 'But he was bloody hopeless at them. It got to the point where my mother used to maybe put a line on on a Saturday and she would whisper to me, "Find out who he's backing." So I would go across and say, "Fancy anything today, Dad?" He'd say, "Two certainties." He always said that. He said, "I'm going to slaughter them today, slaughter them." Then he'd tell me what they were. I'd go and tell my mother and she would put her money on something else. She'd back two others.

'Then there was this day when my mother had had a yankee and the third one up came to the last fence and it was that far ahead that it was from here to Chester. Anyway, it jumps the last and it stumbles and falls. So mother goes, "Blinkin hell." She goes to my dad and she says, "You didn't back that, by any chance, did you?" He just sat there and he wouldn't answer because he was like that – none of your business sort of thing. And she just rounded on him and she said, "You're a jinx." '

Ferguson Snr could not pick a winner, but his son can. The horse that Fergie bought to relieve some of the pressures of managing Manchester United is called Queensland Star after a ship his father helped to build on the Clyde. It won its maiden race at Newmarket, leading from start to finish.

Queensland Star was the first horse to carry Fergie's red and white colours when he lined up for the 4.45 race with West Ham fan Gary Carter in the saddle.

Fergie's four-legged team is made up of a pair of two-year-olds – Queensland Star, trained by Jack Berry near Lancaster, and Candleriggs, which is named after a district of Glasgow and managed by Ed Dunlop in Newmarket – and steeplechaser Yankie Lord, which is with Charlie Brooks at Lambourn.

Fergie is happy to treat the racing game as a hobby and leave the big-match build-up to his trainers. 'I love golf, but I really enjoy racing and it's something my wife Cathy and I can do together,' he said. 'We went to Cheltenham on Gold Cup day last year and that really got us interested. Someone else can have the pressure.'

In football, Ferguson's judgement goes right to the core. He can sense success in a player such as Roy Keane or Peter Schmeichel, but he can sniff out the stench of defeat, too, and in the weeks and months when United slowly let the FA Carling Premiership title drift towards the gratefully outstretched hands of Arsenal, it began to sicken him.

Ferguson detected signs of decay long before the inevitable demise of the title challenge persuaded him that dramatic changes had to be made at Old Trafford. 'There can be complacency in any football club,' Ferguson said. 'Success can bring that. It might not just be in one section of the club. It could be mirrored right through. Maybe we have got to look at our team and ask, "Have we got the same hunger right through the team as we had two years ago?" You have to say that the team of two years ago or the team of '94 would not have lost any of the games we have lost this season.

'There has to be a bit of soul-searching. There are one or two individuals where you have got to say, "Is the hunger the same?" It is very difficult to get it back and we will be making changes at the end of the season, changes in personnel, no matter what the outcome of the League is this season.

'People like myself and the staff and the supporters do not deserve to have it thrown away by the players like this. Not after all the work that has been done here. But the club is like a moving bus. We are not waiting at the stop for anyone who is late and I have always made that point to the players. We have to make sure that the bus goes on now. We cannot stop.

'You could have a knee-jerk reaction and say, "You're all bloody going" – you know what I mean. But the sensible way to do it is to analyse the people with hunger. The ones with the hunger have absolutely no problem here. The ones who are not the same, who have a slight difference in hunger – decisions will be taken on them.

'In the position I am in now, defeat changes me a little bit. I fee losing the League will change me a little bit because I will want to get things done again. That is the great thing about football. It is a never-ending process. You think you have captured it and one little thing can just unship you. It is amazing.'

His own hunger, of course, rages on unabated. His knowledge of United games is encyclopaedic. He could enter any of those trivia quizzes on his team and win every time. Results, substitutions, tackles, passes, goals – the images are locked away in his mind. From last season, the 3–2 defeat away to Coventry City in late December after United had been 2–1 up with three minutes to go, seems particularly vivid in his memory. 'It was absolute suicide,' he said.

But if some of United's recent failings can be attributed to lost appetites Ferguson also acknowledged that the absences of Keane, out since the end of September with a serious knee injury, and Ryan Giggs with a hamstring tear were crucial in stripping United of the fluency and penetration with which they took the Premiership by storm in the early part of the season.

Ferguson said: 'In a situation where you become realistic you have to analyse yourself and analyse your team, and there is no doubt that we have been caught short in lack of quality in terms of the pool of players that we have. The possibility of the loss of Giggs is something we should have done something about at the start of the season. We thought about getting a left-sided player. We tried to buy Blomqvist from AC Milan. They wouldn't sell him but they put him on loan to Parma and they eventually sold him. We should have pushed that through, which would have given us more protection. Instead, we had an imbalance when Giggs eventually went.

'The problem for me is that when my 11 best players are fit it is hard for me to go and take two good players who are the same quality as them. In the case of Blomqvist, you thought he was one that had a chance of being able to play at this club in terms of ability and certain things he has. But if you take him out of the equation where else do you get left-sided players that would at a push fill in for Giggs or allow me to play Giggs in another role? Still, there is no question, we should have done something.

'With Keane, people say, "You have done great; you have not missed Keane." But the games we have lost, we would never have lost them if Keane had been playing. Unfortunately he is not here, but if he had been on the field I think there would have been something different about the place.

'I think there would have been a few angry dressing-rooms at half-time, you know. I think there has been a lack of leadership because of the youthfulness of the team and because some of the foreign players are not used to our type of football.'

Defeat and loss, though, only makes Ferguson come back stronger. There is an air about him already of a man who can hardly wait to put things right, who is rushing towards the future with keen anticipation.

'I have seen success change people overnight and it is not nice,' he said. 'Big-time Charlies, arrogance. They have no time for their roots. I see that in a lot of people. That, to me, is the unacceptable face of football. What I think is the humbling part of football is where you go to games and you see the same managers there all the time and they have been in it for twenty-odd years.

'John Rudge, Dave Bassett and David Pleat. You hold your hand up because they love it, they are in it seriously. They never change. They are still striving for the end of the rainbow. There are people who do not forget their roots.'

The eulogies heaped on Manchester United when they took a seemingly unbeatable Premiership lead earlier last season, and which made a place in the European Cup final an assumed right, were always misleadingly overblown. The strength of their squad proved to be disastrously inadequate by the top European standards to which they aspire.

First, Barnsley knocked them out of the FA Cup in February after losing to them 7–0 at the end of October. That said a lot about Barnsley's fighting spirit but more about United's post-Christmas problems. Then came Monaco, ironically the club which Arsenal's Arsene Wenger once coached. They exposed United's inability to ride out injury problems, specifically the absence of Giggs.

Without Roy Keane they lacked essential bite in midfield, but without Giggs they had no threat of the unexpected and, more prosaically, no width, which tactically has cost them dearly. Expecting David Beckham to provide the breadth, imagination and pace proved to be too much.

When asked why United had recently been less than awesome, several opposing managers whose teams had given them difficult games naturally insisted that there was little wrong. Indeed, Kenny Dalglish even thought that the United side that only drew with his Newcastle were 'as good as ever'. On reflection, though, he said: 'United set the standards but a number of teams have probably caught up with them.' He declined to say whether Arsenal had actually overtaken them in terms of potential, though Joe Kinnear, at Wimbledon, said United were 'no longer out on their own'.

Glenn Hoddle, who suffered from the withdrawals of United players from his England squads, was nevertheless not without sympathy. 'This has been an even more testing season for them than in the past because they've had so many injuries. Everyone wants to take advantage. Everyone tries to raise their game against them, but when you've got injuries you can't rotate the squad to ease the pressure on the ones who are jaded or carrying injuries that need rest.'

Although the increasingly French-orientated Arsenal can contribute some players to the national squad, Hoddle seemed genuinely sorry that United and England are not 'being strong together' in the same way that Ajax and Holland and Bayern Munich and Germany were bonded.

During the World Cup Ferguson managed to find himself in open conflict with the England coach. There had been plenty of suspicion of club versus country conflict between Old Trafford and Lancaster Gate, but once the Finals in France were under way there was no disguising Ferguson's protective instinct towards David Beckham and Hoddle's obsession with the national team's success. Ferguson might have shared an ITV platform with Hoddle but they were at loggerheads and they took a professional view about that 'cosy' relationship, but during the World Cup hostilities erupted over Beckham.

The row warmed up at first when Ferguson expressed his surprise that Darren Anderton should have been included ahead of Beckham in the opening World Cup tie against Tunisia in Marseille, even though he admitted that he tried to sign Anderton from Spurs a few years earlier. While he questioned Anderton's fitness, what upset Hoddle and made the tabloid headlines as extracts from Ferguson's *Sunday Times* column were his remarks about Hoddle's handling of the entire affair.

Ferguson felt that Beckham shouldn't have been exposed to a media press conference to go on TV, radio and in the newspapers, baring his soul about his deep hurt over his exile from the England team at the start of their World Cup campaign. Ferguson would not have permitted Beckham to have been subjected to such scrutiny. A fair enough point. But Hoddle objected to it being made when he was engrossed in the World Cup.

It was also an easy target for the vast array of the communications industry encamped in La Baule close to the England team and hungry for every scrap of headline-making news.

Hoddle was naturally quizzed about Ferguson's *Sunday Times* column and the England coach responded at the media conference at their training camp headquarters in Brittany. He said: 'Whoever makes comments, they are welcome to their own opinions but I'm a bit disappointed. It's not only Alex but I believe there are many people on TV, writing in different papers and on radio making comments, but at the end of the day, chaps, it's my decision. I'm just disappointed that some of these people passing opinions are in the same job as me.' Asked if he would rather they kept quiet, he added, 'Don't put words in my mouth, but I'm sure he's aware of that.'

He was also asked if he had contacted Ferguson. Hoddle said he hadn't. He clearly felt he had more important issues to worry about. Hoddle explained: 'I've got too many things on my mind, too many things to do. But it is unhelpful – put it that way. But then again I look at things different. I'd never put that pressure on Alex before a big European game.'

Would Ferguson appreciate that? Hoddle replied: 'You'd have to ask him that. I can't answer that.'

Later in the day in a live TV link-up Hoddle was far less guarded or diplomatic about his true feelings. Ray Stubbs asked him: 'Glenn, what was your opinion of Alex Ferguson making comments about the way you were looking after David Beckham?'

The precise transcript of Hoddle's response gives an indication of the depth of feeling at the time. 'He's very disappointing as a professional, ya know. If you've got any problems he should have given me a ring. To go into the papers and do it media-wise. I was asked on many occasions before big European games to talk about his team and I declined, quite honestly, because I thought it was the professional thing to do. I understand his problems as coach going into such big games and the eve of going into our game I felt it was unprofessional, but it's his opinion, I'm not going to lose any sleep over it and at the end of the day we all do things differently, don't we?'

Hoddle then indirectly attacked Ferguson for failing to spot a problem with Beckham. Hoddle recognised that Beckham had a lot to cope with, but he said: 'I think that's half of his problems. I don't think he's been focused coming into this tournament at the end of the season, he's not been focused. Perhaps his club should have looked at that a little bit earlier, but he hasn't been focused on his football; he's just been a little vague. We've had a good chat. Whatever other people's opinions of how it was dealt with, we've had a chat. He certainly looks a lot more focused now and came on and did very well for us. He gives us a different option in midfield. He's a great passer of the ball. I love him to bits, 'cos I bought him in, for my first game in Moldova I bought him in. But he's got to understand his football's got to come first, and it's got to remain first, and I felt his focus wasn't there, as an individual, but he's come back very quickly and I think he understands what we're looking for from him.'

Beckham became the centrepiece of the debate over Hoddle's team selection and tactics but, having spotted a flaw, the England coach brought the player into the tournament into central midfield against Colombia – and it worked. However, there was far greater controversy to befall Beckham. His red card in the game against Argentina brought Ferguson and Hoddle head to head again over the same player.

In the national fall-out over Beckham, becoming only the fourth English international to be sent off, Ferguson vowed to protect him from 'mob rule'. He refused to sell Beckham abroad. Beckham would be 'protected', just as Cantona was when he return from his FA exile after the kung-fu kick on a Crystal Palace fan. Cantona had been the target of the hate mob and now Beckham faced the same barracking at every away ground. Clubs in Italy and Spain were ready to swoop like vultures to lure Beckham away from the personal abuse for letting down England with his sending-off against Argentina.

But Ferguson promised to fight back, just as he had with the wayward Frenchman. Selling Beckham abroad 'would be the easy way out' and not an option he planned to take. He explained: 'It would be easy for Manchester United and there are pretty sound reasons for that, but we'll look after the player when he comes back. We'll look after him and he will be protected by Manchester United. That's the kind of club it is. It's a great club and we're not going to give in to the mob rule. No way. David Beckham does not want to leave Manchester United. He's Manchester United through and through. That's the way he is. I always think that when a player comes back after playing for his country he comes back a better player, but on this occasion we'll have a little bit more work to do on David. He'll be down and disillusioned, which will give me a bit of a job to do.'

Ferguson didn't blame Beckham for leaving England as fast as he could once he returned with the England squad from France. He said: 'He wanted to get across the Atlantic Ocean as quick as he could to escape. I've spoken to his mother and she could not believe that when she arrived back from France the media were camped outside David's house with packed lunches and tables! So I know what people say about an open press conference! I think David did absolutely the right thing by going away immediately.'

Ferguson pointed an accusing finger at ITV interviewer Gary Newbon for laying the blame for England's defeat by Argentina on Beckham's sending-off immediately after the game in St Etienne, which set the entire nation against the player. Ironically, in an ITV interview, Ferguson said: 'Glenn was asked an unfortunate question by our friend Gary Newbon on the final whistle. Gary asked Glenn about the sending-off – whether he thought it cost England the game. His natural reaction was to say yes. So Gary stirred a bit of a hornet's nest and everybody ran that the next day. I don't think Glenn meant what he actually said. The question was posed and it was easy to say yes, but he corrected that the next day.'

However, the damage had been done – Beckham became Public Enemy No. 1. He was even the target of a vile attack where fans were encouraged to abuse him at games. A daily newspaper on the Internet launched a sickening editorial suggesting that Beckham didn't know what real pressure was like and that fans should give him the chance to find out by attacking him whenever he played. Under the headline 'It's Our Duty to Taunt Him' the editorial insisted 'it is our patriotic duty to give him hell verbally next season – relentlessly'. Beckham was declared a 'non-person'.

The content of Football365 originates from England and makes its cash from money-spinning advertisers which include Cellnet, computer game World League Soccer 98, various big publishers, Carlsberg, Prime Sports Direct and Zetters. It is listed as Copyright 1998 Direct Network Publishing PLC. The edition of Monday 6 July targeted Beckham in the most despicable and cowardly way possible. This is an extract from one of the worst examples of incitement in any form of the communications industry, described by one reader as 'journalistic hooliganism'.

'Glenn Hoddle, Gareth Southgate, Alex Ferguson, Chris Eubank – they have all called for crowds to lay off David Beckham when he takes to the field for Manchester United next season. Yet surely that is the last thing we should do. Beckham was sent off because he was unable to deal with provocation ... he was too temperamental, too self-centred to think of the good of the team ... Beckham's tantrum was about his own all-too-easily-bruised ego. Gascoigne never grew up, Beckham must ... Clearly we did not taunt him enough. Had Beckham, week in, week out, been subjected to the kind of abuse that surely awaits him next season he would have been hardened against it. Now if we can assist him, Beckham can emerge from this affair a stronger, maturer player. It is our patriotic duty to give him hell verbally next season. Relentlessly. Of course we need to demonstrate some imagination. There is no point in just booing him all the time. He will soon get used to that. Sometimes we need a slow handclap. On other occasions whistles. Or deadly silence. We must make it clear Beckham is a non-person. When he can cope with all this and not run whinging to his manager or agent or Italy then we will know he is up to wearing the Three Lions once more ... He is the most talented midfielder we have. He is also the dumbest. But he is only 23. With our help he can learn.'

The next day came responses from angry readers, which Football365 at least had the guts to publish. Fans from all over the world from Australia to Canada, as well as from England, were deeply shocked. Peter Keddie was quoted on the Internet web site: 'This is journalistic hooliganism. When the crash comes, and come it will, when the foreign footballers have left for the next 'hot spot' you will be left with what you have underneath it all, mediocrity. The better players like Beckham will be gone because of the petty jealous nature and lack of humanity shown by writing like this.' G. Smith, Leicester, wrote: 'This was crass and potentially inflammatory.' Matthew Williams from Toronto, Canada, said: 'Shall we spit in Beckham's face until he hardens? You know, just in case? When Canadians venture to El Salvador in CON-CACAF play the players are regularly pelted with plastic bags filled with urine. So that's why we lose. We haven't become hardened to urine.'

Eddie Small from Perth, Western Australia, said: 'OK, Beckham made a stupid mistake. But when it's all said and done, it's only a bloody game!' Ray McIntosh wrote: 'God only help poor Michael Owen should he ever slip up.' The Internet paper then tried to redress the balance by suggesting that their editorial was not meant to be taken seriously.

The editor of Football365 is Danny Kelly, a close friend of the Danny Baker, Chris Evans and Paul Gascoigne clique, and he has a late night sports show on Channel 5 called 'Under the Moon'.

Kelly tried to hide his embarrassment by claiming the writer penned the attack with 'tongue somewhat in cheek'. It has resulted in 'our biggest ever post bag', admitted Kelly.

However, the damage had already been done and has been little short of an open invitation to sort out Beckham. Governments have tried unsuccessfully so far to regulate the content of the Internet. There has been an alarming increase in football personalities being the subject of some astonishing accusations. Arsenal manager Arsene Wenger was forced to take the extraordinary measure of making an impassioned statement on the steps of Highbury when rumours spread about his personal life after statements appeared on the City Internet. During the World Cup there was some scandalous so-called information about England captain Alan Shearer announced on the Internet.

On the broader issues of the 16th World Cup, Ferguson had much to say. The diving, play-acting, conning, theatricals ... downright cheating. The World Cup was awash with something that used to be taboo inside the professional ranks. Now it was rampant.

Ferguson branded the cheats 'the plague' of the World Cup in France. FIFA's hard-line new instructions to referees has not only protected the artists of the world game, but has encouraged the flagrant con artists. He doesn't condone the retaliation that has made David Beckham a scapegoat for defeat against Argentina, but he doesn't want Argentine captain 'Dirty' Diego Simeone to get away with it.

Ferguson launched the most scathing attack to date on the incompetence of the referees – supposedly the best in the world – to distinguish between the genuine hatchet men and the tricksters. He said: 'The tournament has embraced many great things, but the one plague on the competition is the cheating that goes on in the game. Diving can get a player sent off. The standard of refereeing has been abysmal and that referee in particular was very poor. First and foremost for me it was a bad decision to send David off. David did not dive about, trying to get Simeone sent off – he reacted to what was a bad challenge. David is absolutely devastated by it and so am I by the over-reaction in the media. It was a petty and silly offence and I'm not going to condone it but, having spoken to David, he is not sure whether he was sent off for kicking out at Simeone after what was a nasty challenge or whether it was the aggressive nature he showed to the referee afterwards.'

However, it might even be worse if Beckham got himself sent off for dissent, something he had been warned about time and again by Hoddle and, indeed, Ferguson. But Ferguson's natural defence of one of his own highlights a glaring failure in France for the officials to get a grip. Premiership referees have become much braver in issuing yellow cards to those players who dive inside the box, trying to con a penalty.

In the World Cup the cheats moved all over the pitch, knowing a 9.9 dive would ensure an opponent a booking and that meant a large degree of freedom for the rest of the match.

Ferguson was outraged that Beckham's entire life has now been affected by this one decision. 'I don't think that he deserved to be sent off. It was an innocuous, silly challenge and it was a silly thing for David to do afterwards, and his reaction is something that has happened once or twice before ... but the real crime was the reaction of the English people, which I think is absurd. It's a country that prides itself on justice and fair play and I don't think David deserves the treatment he's had ... Don't you think that David was upset, don't you think that his manager was upset, don't you think that everyone deserves to feel upset at the way England went out on penalties?'

ITV brought Hoddle and Ferguson together for the first time since their dispute over the handling of Beckham's World Cup when the pair were with Terry Venables as the panel of experts for the third and fourth place play-off game between Croatia and Holland in Paris.

ITV might have hoped for a few fireworks but interviewer Tony Francis joked: 'Right, you two, is it time for me and Terry to leave?' Venables couldn't resist a touch of banter at their expense when he chipped in: 'Give 'em the keys to lock up and we'll leave them to it!'

Hoddle wasn't to be outdone as he hit back: 'We had a good fight, a good punch-up, but I wouldn't say who won.' The camera stuck with Hoddle but it would have been nice to have seen Ferguson's expression!

Hoddle and Ferguson talked with Beckham when he returned to pre-season training. Both delivered an identical message – a lecture, a warning and then friendly advice about how to put the red card against Argentina behind him and cope with the new season of club and international football. Hoddle could only communicate by telephone until the England squad regrouped for their opening European Championship match in Sweden, unless he could snatch a few moments with him after a Manchester United game. However, Ferguson had first call on Beckham on a day-to-day basis.

Ferguson insisted he no longer wanted to prolong any row with Hoddle when he said: 'I'm not sore. As far as I'm concerned, it's soon washed over. My view now is that I'm looking forward to seeing David when he gets back in training.' As England coach in a World Cup situation, Hoddle insisted he had the right to make whatever selection he wanted. He said: 'You have to go with your conviction. I felt I made a lot of good decisions. Everyone knows the main part of a manager's job is the ability to make decisions – from what we eat to when we train and who we play. Absolutely everything. That's part of the job I enjoy.'

While Hoddle and Ferguson backed off from a lively Beckham debate, the pair clashed over their differing stances on the World Cup cheats. Ferguson said: 'It has been said that in Europe you cannot win without cheating, and there have been signs of that in the last 30 years with regard to things said about referees. It won't change my philosophy – they have to play by fair means.'

But Hoddle felt if you cannot beat them at their game, you have to join them, and that was indicated by the way the England coach instructed Owen to go down if touched or baulked in the box or around it. Hoddle said: 'My opinion is that if a player gets touched, why shouldn't he go down? We have taken to staying on our feet in our country for far too long. Why should we get 25 free kicks against us per match and only win five?' Venables put his point of view: 'I think we have to stop the culprits, not join them. The way to improve this beautiful game that we all love is not to follow the cheats – we have got to stop the baddies.'

Ferguson concluded: 'FIFA have failed badly. The panel that sits to adjudicate on the players sent off is all wrong. They are not dealing with the real culprits who have tarnished the whole tournament, and that's got to be changed.'

Ferguson and Venables agreed that Holland were one of the outstanding teams. Venables said: 'If Overmars had been fit for the semifinal they could have gone all the way.' Ferguson said: 'Holland had the best shape of all the teams I have seen in the competition but Brazil have Ronaldo and he stands above all the players I've seen.'

United's inability to build on their early-season promise in the European Champions' League goes down to a combination of problems, none of which quite overcome the feeling that they have become profit-motivated at the expense of on-the-field investment. Above all, though, there are the exhausting demands of the Premiership, of which Wenger has regularly complained but about which, through his buying of young players, he has done more than Ferguson to bring relief.

There is a recurring criticism from United fans. They fail to understand why the richest English club seems reluctant to invest the highest amounts on the best available players. In a season that saw the club suffer more injuries than in their previous championship-winning ones, this argument gained greater strength. Only the arrival of money-spinning signings like Stam and Yorke changed the fans' view.

Manchester United PLC and Ferguson do not always see eye to eye on the current prices. The accountants who have such a big say these days point out that while United have become a highly profitable club Real Madrid have bought expensively, put European success above everything and ended up £70 million in debt. But Real Madrid won the European Cup final, and that grates.

Ferguson signed Stam in a bid to find a central defensive partnership capable of underpinning his bid for European success. The Dutch international joined United for £10.75 million, a world record fee for a defender, and Ferguson was delighted to have clinched the deal after a month of negotiations. 'Jaap Stam is a world-class defender. I don't think there's any doubt about that. It's what we need right now and I'm very pleased that, subject to the formalities, we've finally got him. He's a terrific defender who is quick and who can pass the ball and I'm sure he'll do well for us.'

United have never adequately replaced Steve Bruce, their inspirational captain, who left after leading them to a League and Cup Double. Phil and Gary Neville and Norwegians Ronny Johnsen and Henning Berg have all been used to partner or replace injury-plagued Gary Pallister without ever looking rock-solid. Ferguson knows that to have any chance of regaining the Premier League title as well as achieving his cherished dream of winning the European Cup he must have defenders capable of stopping the likes of Ronaldo and Alessandro del Piero. 'It's fair to say that we've had to change our centre backs quite a lot – more often than we'd like – but Stam will certainly be a great addition,' Ferguson said. 'We have to be stronger to handle everything that's involved with domestic and European football, and bringing in players like Stam will only help us. There could be more teams in the European Cup next year and that would mean something like ten group games. That puts a tremendous pressure on your resources so we need to be ready.'

The 25-year-old international said after winning the Dutch footballer of the year award that he had always wanted to play for the English champions. Stam had been contracted to play for the Eindhoven club until 2003 and PSV had put a $28 million price tag on him before finally agreeing to a reduced fee. Stam, who won the Dutch League Cup and Supercup with PSV, began his professional career at the comparatively late age of 19, playing for FC Zwolle, Cambuur Leewarden and Willem II Tilburg before moving to Eindhoven. His international debut came as a substitute against Germany in 1996 but he made his name in a friendly against Brazil where he was impressive in the air and in his marking of Ronaldo. 'Stam's a real pro, he's very fast and he's a good header,' Glasgow Rangers coach Dick Advocaat said. 'It's a very good thing for United. He's a real team player and one of the best defenders in the world.' Several English clubs showed an interest in Stam after he said he wanted to play in the Premier League. The previous most expensive defender was Spain's Roberto Rios who moved to Athletic Bilbao from Real Betis two years ago for the huge sum of £9 million.

Not even a world record for a defender will pacify the fans for whom a defender, however good, is not a potential star in the 'Theatre of Dreams'.

Ferguson resolved one major problem, but still has the biggest headache to cure at Old Trafford. Stam provides the defensive might for another assault on the Champions' League, but Ferguson has failed to replace Eric Cantona.

Teddy Sheringham was recruited almost as an afterthought when he became available at Spurs. A modest £3.5 million fee was worth the gamble. It hasn't paid off. Old Trafford is left with an uncharacteristically empty trophy cabinet. Sheringham has never won a major trophy in his career – apart from the Charity Shield!

Ferguson's latest attempt to bring the European Cup back to Old Trafford needs an inspirational figure. Although Cantona was sometimes a let-down in the big European games, on other occasions he was light years ahead.

An interesting fact is that the last time United collected a trophy without Cantona was back in 1992 – the League Cup.

It may be that Cantona is irreplaceable. Maybe Ferguson knew it. Fergie had the chance to buy Marcelo Salas from River Plate for £12 million but opted out of purchasing the Chilean goalscorer at that price. He's been linked with a succession of world superstars, including

Alessandro del Piero, who is valued at the Ronaldo-style £50 million package. If Ferguson is to prove that Cantona is not irreplaceable then it is going to cost close to double the price paid for Stam.

Little wonder he chased Eric over to France to persuade him to return after the FA extended his ban to reserve games. Little wonder Ferguson stood by him after his kung-fu kick on a Crystal Palace fan. Certainly he cannot do with any more cut-price players. He's got to land the big one to generate fresh conviction for the fans that there really is life after Eric.

Ferguson was undoubtedly convinced that Arsenal would buckle under the weight of their fixture list. Gradually he became increasingly irritated that his prediction underestimated Arsenal and his own problems of turning United into the team of international standing that so recently was all too confidently predicted.

The United boss opened up on the agony of seeing his side dethroned as kings of English football by awesome Arsenal, but he banished any misgivings about his future as United saw off bitter rivals Leeds in their final home match. Fergie outlined his blueprint for claiming the title back from the Gunners in his programme notes.

'We will gather strength from the setbacks of this season,' he said. 'Disappointment is part of football and part of growing up. We are a young club and we will learn from our mistakes. So many of our players have not reached their prime yet. Their best is yet to come and they will get over the knocks that fate has handed us this season. As I reflect on the twists and turns of this season, I can't wait to get started again. I am determined to be there and see these players fulfil their great promise. I will look into where we went wrong and examine my own contribution. We must all stand up and be counted. I don't like failing – none of us do – and we intend to do something about it.'

Stam watched United cruise to victory over Leeds United ahead of completing his move and signing a seven-year contract, and he is in no doubt about the status of the club he is joining. He said: 'It's a shame that United are not champions this season. But they will be next year – I'm absolutely sure of that. It is a dream to come here. I simply couldn't wait to get inside the ground. Everything has been so special for me – the crowd, the stadium and the team. There are so many great players out there, but Ryan Giggs is something else – he didn't give Leeds a chance.'

Ferguson added: 'I have a group of young players who have never known defeat before. They have won everything on their way up from the youth ranks and have even played for their country. Now they know the meaning of defeat, and it's a question of how they react to it. They can wither and die or make sure they don't have to go through it again. I'm hungry for more success next season and I'm sure they will be, too.'

United's England defender Gary Neville answered Fergie's challenge by saying: 'We had our sights on the title and the European Cup at the start of the season, and it hurts that we've missed out. We have to put it right next season – and that means bringing the championship back to Old Trafford.'

He is sure his side will bounce back after missing out on their third successive Premiership title and will have no problem dealing with the setback of finishing second to Arsenal. 'We've experienced losing the League before but I haven't experienced losing it with two games to go. It usually goes to the last game of the season. It is not new, losing the League – we lost the Double within a week. We have lost European Cup semi-finals and quarter-finals.

'There have been big disappointments in the three or four years I have been playing at this level so it is not as if there have not been any upsets. It is a case of how you bounce back from them. People say you sometimes learn more when you lose rather than when you win. We know we've got to put a show on for our fans. It is essential that we go out on a high note because we haven't given our fans the showing they deserve since perhaps the first hour against Chelsea in the FA Cup in January.' The England full back praised Arsenal for their success and said: 'They have been unbelievable and have won so many games on the trot you cannot argue about what they have done.'

Ferguson was delighted to give even more youngsters like defender Wes Brown his debut against Leeds before the end of the season. The England youth international is the latest home-grown talent to emerge off the Old Trafford production line and the 18-year-old has been likened to Paul McGrath. 'I toyed with the idea of starting him from the beginning,' said Ferguson, 'but I thought it would be better to bring him on with the support of the crowd behind him because I know how much they appreciate young players at this club. He's still got a bit of meat to put on the bone and I've great hopes for him.'

Ferguson has launched into world record signings, but his development of young talent has been equally spectacular. Beckham, Scholes,

Butt and the Neville brothers have been examples of success stories of home-grown talent emerging at the same time.

The Manchester United boss used his powers of psychology to transform David Beckham from a shy, skinny kid to an England World Cup star, albeit a highly controversial one. His feet were not just kept on the ground in his early days – they were virtually nailed down. Just when he thought he would make it, Beckham would find himself cast back in the shadows with all the other wannabees.

He remembers: 'The first time I really got into the squad the manager wasn't using me a lot. I was on the bench and sometimes I wasn't even getting changed. That kept me hungry. I always wanted to be there. And once I got a taste for it, I felt sort of embarrassed if I wasn't there. When I got to Manchester I didn't want people down in London saying, "Oh, he'll be back in a couple of years because he's crap." And I was worried they would also be saying that I hadn't made the standard. It was a sort of an embarrassment.'

Beckham first unveiled his skills as a kid at White Hart Lane until Tottenham decided he was too lightweight to make it big. But after winning a Bobby Charlton school of excellence award, Beckham was on his way north to join the club he had supported as a kid. He stepped out of his Leytonstone home in east London and into Old Trafford as a teenage stranger. He had to wait before he was introduced to the big time and a debut against Leeds at Old Trafford in April 1995.

It was then that Beckham found out just how tough it was to survive in the mood-swinging world of Fergie. When Becks thought he was in, he was out. And being farmed off to Preston on loan did not exactly fill him with confidence about establishing a United career.

He revealed in *Arena* magazine: 'The boss certainly gives you confidence – but he doesn't give you too much of it. He can bring you into the first team for training for two days on the trot. And then for two weeks you won't be training with the first team again. That was how it went. But, as I say, that's what kept me hungry...'

Perhaps eventual 'retirement' from the front line as manager of Manchester United might convince Ferguson to have a second crack at international management. He played a role in Scotland's World Cup build-up, running the rule over all the Scots' Group A opponents – holders Brazil, Norway and Morocco. His views featured in an hour-long STV documentary on the World Cup. Then he handed his dossier over to Craig Brown, giving the Scotland boss an invaluable insight.

Ferguson, who was Scotland's caretaker boss at Mexico '86 after Jock Stein died, also saw Brazil beat Germany 2–1. He was also to be in Copenhagen to see Norway's match against Denmark and travelled to Casablanca to see Glenn Hoddle's England against Morocco.

Brown said: 'Alex's knowledge of the game is invaluable. I remember visiting him at United's training ground last year, and he showed me one of his most prized possessions. It was a photograph of United's 1992 youth team, nine of whom have gone on to become full internationals.' The producer of *The Ferguson Files*, Ross Wilson, said: 'Alex's experience will be crucial. He is a master tactician and he spots invaluable things during the course of a game which I'm sure Craig will be taking on board.'

Juventus superstar and French inspirational World Cup forward Zinedine Zidane believes that United will eventually win the European Cup. Before Juve faced Monaco in the Champions' League, knowing it might have been Manchester United in their semi-final, he argued: 'They are the best European team we have faced this season.' United stunned Juventus in a 3–2 victory at Old Trafford in October, and although they went down 1–0 in their second Champions' League meeting, Zidane felt Juventus were lucky to escape and qualify for the later stages.

In a glowing tribute to the English champs, he said: 'I am sure one day they will go on to win the European Cup. They were incredible at Old Trafford and so hard to break down when we met in Turin. We all realise just how fortunate we were to make it into the quarter-finals. They could easily have knocked us out. I believe their time will come. Their young players will simply get better and better. They should not feel despondent in losing to Monaco. I'm sure if they had been at full strength they would have gone through. We could so easily have been meeting them once again.'

Zidane believed the crushing blows of losing Ryan Giggs and Peter Schmeichel for the quarter-final sealed United's fate. He said: 'Giggs was brilliant against us at Old Trafford. We simply had no answer to him. He showed us he is a truly world-class player. Schmeichel was magnificent in Turin and his absence was always going to be a crucial factor against Monaco. But if it's any consolation, United's form this season in the Champions' League has made a lot of people sit up and take notice. And I am sure they will be even stronger next season. Players like the Neville brothers, Nicky Butt, Paul Scholes and David Beckham will only improve in time. But they showed against us and in their other Champions' League games a remarkable maturity for such young men.'

Ferguson has won every domestic honour both sides of the border, with a couple of European Cup Winners' Cups thrown in. One former Dons player says: 'We found it difficult to handle sometimes. All the stuff about tea-cups flying is true. He would rant and rave, then he would go into the lounge. We'd come in and he'd be charming the wives, and chatting away as if nothing had happened.'

He is the type to remember what he sees as a slight. He once accused a group of journalists of cheating during a pop quiz on an Aberdeen Euro trip.

Ferguson is simply uncompromising. He even sold his own son!

Darren Ferguson played for Manchester United and then was sold by his dad. His wife Cathy observed after United's first championship win: 'I could not believe how cooly he took everything. He really is a changed man since we came south of the border. When he was manager of Aberdeen, Alex was really hard to live with . . . but not any longer.'

Ferguson says: 'I have a ruthless streak, and I don't like myself for it. It's always there, and has been since I started management at Aberdeen. I'll do anything for my players. If they were to wake me at 5 a.m. in the morning and ask for a lift somewhere, I'd pick them up. But, then, don't ask me to be loyal when I have to pick my team. The loyalty I have then is to the club.' He also said: 'Winning means keeping your job, and it can be a delicate situation. But I tell myself I'm not going to fail in this game. It means making unpopular decisions, but I don't want the chairman coming up to me and saying it's time to call it a day.'

George Graham, when he was the Arsenal boss, once brawled with Ferguson in the tunnel at Old Trafford. Graham said: 'People say I'm ruthless. That's their opinion but I don't think I am. I remember when Alex first came down to take over at United. I had never met him and I was dying to find out all about this manager who had done so well in Scotland. Arsenal got beaten. We ended up fighting in the tunnel, and slagging each other off. But I don't know why Scots managers are so successful. Maybe it's because of our passion for the game – part of the Scottish character. I know what motivates me – the little brown envelopes that come through your letter box each morning – bills.'

The two men were born just eleven miles apart in Glasgow, and fought for everything that came their way. Graham goes on: 'It's all very well people philosophising about the game, but I don't know anything else other than football. Sometimes you have to make decisions that are very hard. I know it makes me unpopular, but I hope players thank me afterwards. I push them, and that's to make sure they won't have any regrets in five years' time, or when they finish.'

Lee Martin, a forgotten star shown the door by Ferguson, says: 'My move to Celtic means I'm still one of the most successful of the young players who came through under Alex Ferguson. At a club like Man United you have to take your chances. If you get a game you *must* produce and then hopefully get a run of five or six matches. I don't blame Alex Ferguson for it – he did his best for all of us. When I came to Celtic I phoned Alex and he said he'd always be there if I needed advice.'

Ferguson has a stormy relationship with the media, whether television, radio or the written press. He called Jimmy Hill a prat for having a go at Eric Cantona. One newsman accused Ferguson of inventing the word 'paranoia'. It's little wonder that his public image is so poor. He has many enemies in the press, and those he has crossed swords with have little inclination to try to rectify his image.

Ferguson is top of the popularity stakes at Old Trafford, but for football fans in the rest of the country he's the man they most love to hate – the runaway winner of a poll organised by *Total Football* magazine to find the most unpopular person in British soccer. Ferguson polled 34% of the total votes cast, with fans citing jealousy of his success and what they see as his paranoia with other people within the game as reasons for disliking the Scot. Graham Taylor was second with 13% of the 1,500 or so votes, with most supporters seemingly unwilling to forgive him for England's failure to qualify for the 1994 World Cup finals in the United States. Two relative newcomers to the British game – beleaguered Tottenham boss Christian Gross and Fulham owner Mohammed Al Fayed – found their way into the top ten, while perennial hate figure Jimmy Hill is a surprisingly lowly ninth.

Words were exchanged when Dalglish pulled out of Scotland's World Cup squad in 1986. Ferguson, still Aberdeen manager, had taken on the Scotland job after Jock Stein's death at Cardiff. Ferguson was pinning his faith on Dalglish, not only as a player but as a man running a much more prominent club than Aberdeen.

Then, one night shortly before the Finals, came a bolt from the blue. Dalglish phoned Ferguson at home and said he was withdrawing from the squad. Ferguson was livid. He had to get in his car and drive around to cool down. He phoned a close friend, still seething. 'I can't believe it,' said Ferguson. 'He's really the only guy we have who can do anything special, and now he's gone.' Dalglish pulled out because of a knee injury. In the papers the following day, he explained: 'Unless I rest the knee and hardly bend it over the next three weeks, the damage could be more serious. I phoned Alex Ferguson right away. I feel terrible, not for myself but for him. He has done so much for me this season.' Ferguson pointed out that others were willing to go to the World Cup in Mexico after a hard season. Angry words were exchanged – not for the first time that year. Dalglish disagreed with Ferguson over his decision to leave out Alan Hansen, Dalglish's Liverpool skipper. Ferguson had favoured his successful Aberdeen defensive pairing of Alex McLeish and Willie Miller. There were suggestions that Hansen would play in midfield, but they never came to anything and Hansen was left out of the squad. Hansen refused to comment. Asked about the relationship between Ferguson and Dalglish, he said: 'I just don't want to get involved in any of that.' According to some, Ferguson has never forgotten Dalglish's World Cup withdrawal.

In April 1988, as Liverpool won the title again and Ferguson was struggling at United, the teams drew 3–3 but Ferguson, furious at the dismissal of defender Colin Gibson, was in the tunnel complaining about referee intimidation at Anfield. Dalglish, carrying his six-week-old daughter, interrupted the radio interview and suggested that the journalist talk to the babe-in-arms rather than the United manager. 'My daughter talks more sense than you do,' he said to Ferguson. The United boss was offended. 'I now understand why clubs come away from here biting their tongues and choking on their vomit, knowing that they have been done by referees.'

But there has been the odd olive branch proffered. According to one Premiership manager, Ferguson was quick to offer sympathy after Hillsborough. 'Alex was the first on the phone to Kenny after Hillsborough. They may be great rivals but there are times when these things must be set aside.' One former team-mate of Dalglish said: 'We all knew they never got on. It really started with the World Cup back in 1986 when Fergie was in charge of Scotland. Kenny would never say it in the dressing room to gee players up for a game, but we always felt he was particularly keen to beat Manchester United.

'Once a fan had a go at Ron Atkinson, then United boss, with a canister of CS gas, and we tried to ease the tension next time round. Bob Paisley was to travel on their bus, Bobby Charlton on ours. Fergie, by this time in charge, came in to do a radio interview in Liverpool with Kenny. But when Dalglish realised Fergie was going, he sent another player along. There's no love lost.'

Another former team-mate recalls pulling Kenny and Souness apart in the dressing room. 'They just both wanted to win so much. Maybe it's the same with Fergie and Kenny. Maybe it's because they're Scottish.'

Ferguson was furious at TV pundit Andy Gray for suggesting a spot-kick should have been awarded against United. Gray defended his comments and claimed that he had received a lot of mail from viewers who felt he was biased in favour of the champions. 'Alex should actually see my mail that arrives at Sky from others around the country who think I'm so biased towards Manchester United that I shouldn't be doing the job. I can see what Alex is saying, but it was my opinion, and he might not agree, but it won't be the first time Alex and I haven't agreed.'

Yet for all the encounters of confrontation, rows and raised voices, even those who have been on the receiving end still hold Ferguson in great affection and high esteem. Inside the inner sanctum of his friends and associates there is always a tale or two of angry words often followed by a deep relationship or everlasting resentment. There is little middle ground with Ferguson. They love him or hate him.

Nobby Stiles lived the Manchester United legend as part of Sir Matt Busby's United super-team that beat Benfica to win the European Cup at Wembley in 1968. Stiles says: 'I have watched United since I was a kid. I signed for them when I was 15. They've been my life. I adored the Busby Babes and I believe that the similarities between Alex's side and Sir Matt's team are unmissable. You have the Neville brothers, Phil and Gary, Paul Scholes, Nicky Butt and Giggsy. I am totally biased when it comes to the Reds, of course!'

Emotions were running high in Manchester in the year that saw the 40th anniversary of the Munich air crash. 'Everything Alex's team does reminds me of Denis Law, Paddy Crerand and George Best in the sixties. The reason why it'll all come good is Alex Ferguson. He has unlimited desire and that *has* to be passed on to his players. Or else!'

To separate Ferguson from Busby is a delicate business, but Stiles has a diplomatic solution. 'For me, Sir Matt was the hardest of all acts to follow. Who knows what amazing things he might have achieved if the

Babes' lives had been spared? But Alex has built his own reputation at Old Trafford. And it would only be a fitting tribute to his work if United won the European Cup.'

Comparisons are continually drawn between the 1968 side and the current team. Stiles understands why, but for him there are greater similarities with the Busby Babes. 'I look at the current United side, and they remind me most of the 1957–8 side because so many of them are so young. I see David Beckham, Nicky Butt, Gary and Phil Neville and Paul Scholes, and it reminds me of those players. The 1968 side that I played in was different in that Sir Matt had to bring in players from outside, like Denis Law and Paddy Crerand, so it was not a side that had grown up together in the same way. There's a freshness and vitality about this side which was the same as the 1957–8 side.'

Manchester United has achieved a mastery over the domestic game this decade but since ending their 26-year championship drought in 1993, the Old Trafford side's European excursions have brought a series of unfulfilled desires. Gary Neville made the point just before United exited against Monaco. He said: 'We want to become a great side and to be looked upon as one. But the fact is that all the great sides of the past have won the European Cup. Until we win this trophy we won't be looked upon in that light, can't be compared well with those teams. That's why it's so important that we do it. Europe is special to this club, and the pressure is on us to better ourselves, to take that next step and win it.'

The big let-down was the inhibited performance in Monaco. It was against Ferguson's natural inclination to sacrifice freedom of expression in favour of rigid, defensive discipline.

'It was an unusual directive from me but my younger players do not possess the tactical mind at the present time to sit back and ensure they do not lose the ball and leave themselves open to being counter-attacked,' Ferguson explained. 'When they get involved in the flow of the game there is a danger of them getting carried away. It is extremely difficult for me to put the reins on them but it was absolutely necessary to ensure the right result. I was insistent in what I wanted. I took a lot of care in explaining to them why I wanted them to stray from our usual style. The unpredictability of the playing surface in Monaco demanded we had to sacrifice our offensive momentum and the rhythm of our passing game. I didn't like doing it, but the end justified the means in this case. I have seen Monaco in previous games when they appeared to be subdued, only to contrive a goal out of nothing. It would have been nice, of course, to have got a goal ourselves, and the reason I was disturbed about the absence of Giggs was because he has been in brilliant form and was capable of winning the game off his own bat.'

Ferguson admitted that his unusual course of action was fashioned by defeat at the semi-final stage when United tumbled despite dominating Borussia Dortmund, the eventual surprise winners of the European Cup. 'Everyone was telling me then how unlucky we had been. But we lost that first leg because we allowed our midfield to be spread all over the place when they scored their goal. I was determined it was not going to happen in Monaco. I know the players did not enjoy the way we had to play but they can save their enjoyment for the Old Trafford return.'

On 7 September 1998 came the announcement that Rupert Murdoch's BSkyB had made a £623.4 million take-over offer for Manchester United. Ferguson acknowledged that this might be worrying news for United fans, but had this to say: 'I will state categorically that our supporters know full well that we've always considered them to be a major part of this club. Anything that is allowed to happen to this club must for the good of the supporters, otherwise it won't go ahead. The fans can rest assured they will be considered. And they can rest assured that anything that does happen will not be detrimental to the team.'

Chairman Martin Edwards also attempted to reassure worried fans. Edwards was to join the Sky board as part of the Old Trafford revolution, but as a storm of protest raged from supporters' clubs and politicians, the chairman and chief executive insisted that there had been no betrayal. 'I believe what we have done will strengthen Manchester United, not weaken us. We have not betrayed Manchester United's fans, we have given them a brighter future.'

Edwards denied that the deal had been personally agreed with Rupert Murdoch. 'I never met Rupert Murdoch before or after the deal. He [Murdoch] has a 40% stake in Sky and he is one of 17 directors. All my negotiations have been with Mark Booth [Sky's chief executive].'

Edwards pledged that he would not do anything to harm a club he has followed for 40 years. He said: 'There could be a fear factor among the fans. But what they will see is the club will be run exactly the same as it has been for the last 18 years.' He was confident that in time the hostility towards it would wear off. 'Clearly some supporters are not happy with things and we are not necessarily going to turn them around very quickly. They will make their own judgments in time. If they woke up and found Sky had taken over Arsenal or Liverpool or any other club they might be very disappointed. They might have thought we had missed a trick.' Edwards warned that take-overs of football clubs by huge media concerns will be a feature of the new millennium. 'We would rather be first. Manchester United has always been first.'

Sky's chief executive, Mark Booth, described the United management as 'superb' and said: 'When you take the best broadcasters and the best football club and put them together that is the magical combination.' The role of Murdoch was the subject of much debate, but Ferguson admitted he had had no dealings with the media tycoon. Of Murdoch, he said: 'I don't know him. You've got to know people before you can have views on them.'

In a heartfelt appeal to the fans, Ferguson said: 'The supporters who follow this club know that all the players love Manchester United, and they know that I do myself. We are Manchester United to the core. The players have proved how much they feel for this club by signing new contracts at a young age and committing themselves. They have just got on with it in training, despite all the take-over talk. We are cut off from it all, and the supporters will recognise that.'

Meanwhile, Sir Roland Smith, chairman of the United PLC board, said Sky would not interfere in team affairs and transfer policy. 'Alex Ferguson will be in charge of team selection. Alex Ferguson and the board of Manchester United will be responsible for the acquisition of new players.' Smith added that ticket prices for matches at United's Old Trafford home would not be affected by the bid. He stressed that the current United management team of chief executive Martin Edwards, his deputy Peter Kenyon and finance director David Gill would continue to oversee the day-to-day running of the club.

In the offer document Smith wrote that the proposed deal did not mean that United games would be screened only on a pay-per-view basis – noting that Sky was committed to showing 60 games per season on its existing subscription services. He pointed out that United had no right of veto in respect to the future sale of rights by the 20 clubs in the Premier League. The current Sky contract runs until 2001.

Ferguson was clearly seen as a vital ingredient of the Sky take-over.

He was offered a three-year extension to his current contract, putting him in the £1 million-a-year bracket.

Ferguson's decision to carry on into his sixties as boss had some bearing on his assistant Brian Kidd's decision, late in 1998, to succeed sacked Roy Hodgson as the Blackburn Rovers manager. The club tried to persuade Kidd to stay on by dangling a new contract in front of him – even though he only signed a four-year deal in the summer. Edwards insisted that Kidd's decision to leave Old Trafford after twenty years' service as a player and coach had nothing to do with money. 'Brian's decision was clearly not about money. We did offer Brian more money. We offered him a substantial package to stay at Old Trafford, but it became very obvious that this had nothing to do with his remuneration. The simple fact is Brian wanted to become number one.'

Kidd's departure came when United were facing a match against Aston Villa at the top of the Premiership and just about to play Bayern Munich, with a quarter-final place at stake in the Champions' Cup. 'That's why it's difficult to take because we are in the middle of a really important programme for the club,' Ferguson said. 'I would have preferred it to have been in the summer to be honest with you. I worked hard in the summer to keep him here and we are all disappointed that he has left.'

Fergie, who promoted reserve boss Jim Ryan to the position of care-taker assistant, said: 'We're disappointed Brian's left, it's never easy to think about the break-up after seven years, but that's the nature of football and Manchester United have to look ahead. The one thing you can never underestimate is a person's ambition, you have to encourage it, and in Brian's case he felt that was time to try management on his own. He has been a good servant to me and we have had a good relationship.'

Ferguson then began the task of looking for Kidd's successor. He said: 'Obviously it is an important role, given the size of the job nowadays, and we will have to give it a great deal of consideration to bring in the right person. You need an assistant who can take the responsibility of looking after players, in particular the training sessions, and now that relationship has to be reassembled. That's part of the challenge of football, like when the team broke up in '94, or when we lost Cantona or when Schmeichel announced he is retiring at the end of the season. Then we had to rebuild and this is what we have to do now.'

There will never be another Alex Ferguson. His total hands-on style of management and coaching is a throwback to the golden eras of Sir Matt Busby, Bill Shankly and Bill Nicholson. That became clear from the man himself as he reflected on an Old Trafford career that began 12 years earlier on 6 November 1986, the day after Ron Atkinson was sacked, and when United were bottom of the old First Division. He was asked if anyone coming into the tough world of modern-day management would last his 12 years.

Ferguson, smiling, said: 'No. No, I can't see that. I am the last of the dying breed. Yes, a dying breed, not a dinosaur. You won't see someone coming in again and doing a hands-on job like this. That won't happen either here or anywhere else. It's too difficult. It's too vast. Blimey, we have more staff here than Marks and Spencers.'

Did he feel that he was close to perfection in the form of the 1998 team that took Europe by storm?

'Perfection?' he repeated. 'The only thing that's perfect with me is my perseverance. It's just like a game of golf. You play one great game and then the next you are left disappointed.

'When my team is playing the way it is at the moment the big challenge is to keep it going, particularly with important games coming up like Barcelona away and Bayern Munich at home. I have got five weeks to maintain a real good standard of football. I have to ensure we get to the Champions' League quarter-finals first of all and then keep our place at the top of the Premiership. The job here is to try to maintain standards. If the players can create their own and they have a pride in that, a self-motivation, a self-preparation, then the job is much easier. You have to accept that's the way it is. Maintaining standards and a level of commitment.'

Will that motivation wane even in Ferguson one day?

'It's not a question for me to answer,' he replies. 'I just carry on. And anyway you don't become stale even after 12 years. You can't be stale at a club like this. There is always something happening. Always something you have to turn your hand to.'

Ferguson is undoubtedly the greatest silverware collector of the 1990s, but throughout I wondered if he harboured any regrets about those glory years.

'There's no point in regretting anything,' he said. 'You can maybe make a mistake here, a mistake there. But you can't look upon them as something to regret. You might want to do one or two things again if you had the chance. Maybe changed your mind about something. But nothing serious. Not serious enough to regret.'

He added: 'I'm not envious of anyone starting the job, except perhaps of the money they will be earning. Anyway in four or five years I hope to be still managing. So someone will have to match that for 15 or 16 years.' The laughter kicked in now as he joked: 'Maybe it won't be here. You never know. Maybe I will go and manage Brondby with big Schmeichel in goal at 41 years of age. But really, the time has flown. You wonder where the 12 years have gone sometimes. The high point? Winning the League for the first time. That really opened the door for us. We had waited 26 years for it to happen. Since then the club has got stronger. I don't really think, though, that 12 years here is a special landmark. It's been a long time and there have been some great players at Old Trafford. I've enjoyed it, yes. But there's still work to be done...'

He insisted that he has no notion of retiring, and instead is concentrating on what he does best – winning trophies. 'I don't think I'll do another 12 years, but there is more damage to be done.'

Characteristically, Ferguson treated the anniversary just like any other day during his long and successful reign. No champagne or an extra hour in bed, and he was at the Cliff training ground bright and early as usual. 'Why should I?' he asked. 'There's work to be done and we've got a game on Sunday,' he said, adding jokingly, 'I'll celebrate when I finally leave.'

MILESTONES

6 November 1986: Ferguson appointed United manager.

January 1990: Mark Robins' winner at Nottingham Forest in the FA Cup third round is widely credited with saving Ferguson's job.

May 1990: Lifts his first trophy at Old Trafford when United beat Crystal Palace in the FA Cup Final replay.

May 1991: United win the European Cup Winners' Cup.

April 1992: United win the League Cup, but lose title race to Leeds.

October 1992: Pulls off a masterstroke when he signs Eric Cantona, who proves to be the missing piece in his Championship jigsaw.

May 1993: United win the inaugural Premiership crown, ending their 26-year wait for the title.

May 1994: Guides the club to their first League and Cup Double.

May 1996: His unwavering support for Eric Cantona following his infamous kung-fu attack pays off as the Frenchman inspires United to a record-breaking second Double.

May 1997: United win Premiership title number four.

THE EARLY YEARS

Chris Anderson

Former vice-chairman of Aberdeen

Chris Anderson was regarded as the most far-sighted Scottish football administrator of his generation. Shortly before his untimely death from motor neurone disease in 1987 he recollected, in this previously unpublished account, how the club had set about revitalising itself to meet the challenges of the newly inaugurated Scottish Premier Division and move into the most successful era of its history.

Under Alex Ferguson, Aberdeen won all of the Scottish domestic honours and the Cup Winners' Cup, a feat he was to repeat at Old Trafford. In retrospect it can be seen that the vision of the Aberdeen board prepared Fergie for the challenges he would face subsequently at Old Trafford.

'For a very long period of the club's history we were a comfortable but not a dominant outfit and I think it is fair to say that we were not alone in that respect. Most of the city clubs in Scotland occupied an undemanding position in the Scottish league. There was a fat middle and Aberdeen were there along with Hibs, Hearts, Dundee and Dundee United. It didn't matter a great deal whether you were near the top of the League because you weren't going to be bottom.

'The creation of the Premier Division in 1975 changed all that because it was really a seeded competition and we were very nearly relegated in its first season. We survived only on goal difference and I have to say that the experience was a genuine shock for us and it made us think about what kind of club we should be, which in turn caused us to look very carefully – certainly more methodically than any other club at that time – at what kind of team we should have and what kind of manager should be in charge of that team.

'We decided to clear the decks. Everything was examined – the stadium, the way we treated our supporters, the expectations our players should have at this club. At the same time the city of Aberdeen was experiencing an extraordinary transformation because of North Sea oil. We had become the oil capital of Europe, and for a city based on farming and fishing – which were profitable but very insular – it was an intimidating experience but also an exciting time.

'So the city and its club were both faced with unprecedented challenges. At Pittodrie we decided that we shouldn't just look for whatever manager was available. For the first time in our history we thought we should draw up a profile of the kind of individual who could take us onwards.

'And we quickly realised that one man wouldn't fit the bill completely, so we decided to look for the person who could see us through each stage of our development. First of all we needed to sell ourselves to the public and to the rest of the football world, so we brought in Ally McLeod. He came in 1975 and won the Scottish League Cup more or less right away. His whole attitude was magical. He breathed new life into us and the city and everybody was dancing on air. Ally insisted to the players that we could be successful and that was the start of the process.

'When he left to take charge of Scotland we decided that we now had a base to build on and that we should have somebody with a track record as a player. That man was Billy McNeill, and although we didn't win any honours with Billy it was clear that we were becoming steadily more substantial as a club. After little more than a season Celtic asked him to replace Jock Stein, which was an invitation and an honour he couldn't refuse.

'We were in the position where we were regarded as breeding managers. Scotland had taken Ally McLeod – too soon, we believed – and Celtic had taken Billy McNeill. The next stage was for us to become a club where it would not be just a matter of someone else turning up and making our manager an offer and he would want to leave. We wanted to make our manager think twice about leaving but, of course, that manager would have to take the club into the situation where that could happen.

'We analysed it clinically and coldly and we could see that Alex Ferguson was a man who fitted our profile. In football, as in almost every other walk of life, success can come to seem an inevitable process when you look back on it, but there were many, many people – and there were some in the game who said this to us – that thought we were daft and crazy to appoint Alex Ferguson. But we didn't need someone with a great record as a player; we needed a manager with an abundant and wide knowledge of the game – a top coach.

'You see, we knew we now had a firm base and we believed it was vital to have a manager who had refined coaching and technical abilities. That man, the one with all the warts about him at that time, was Alex Ferguson. We had watched his progress with St Mirren, observed his huge vitality and realised that although he had ended up fighting a messy industrial tribunal with the club after he was sacked, in fact, his energy and commitment had overwhelmed them.

'We were confident in our judgement of him and although we did feel that it might take a bit of time for him and us to be on the same wavelength we were sure that Fergie would do the job for us. And he came here very humble – which might surprise people but only those who really don't know him – because we had rescued him from a rough time he was going through. The bad publicity he got then was putting other clubs off the idea of offering him a job. Our feeling was that he wasn't too much of a handful for them, but rather that they weren't big enough for him.

'The first thing we did was distract him from the World Cup in Argentina and take him to America because there were aspects of American sports management which we felt he would respond to and which suited our position at that time. One of the first things I said to Fergie was, "How would you like to come to the States with me to have a look around?"

'And his eyes opened wide and he said, "Sure! Will I need a passport?" So that was sorted out and off we went, and he was bubbling over with ideas by the time we got back. The American trip energised him – not that Fergie has ever really needed that – but it was important for him, I think, because it rehabilitated him. By the time he came back he had put the St Mirren affair in perspective and he saw that what mattered was the future and that now he had a club and a board who would support him, who would encourage him.

'I have often wondered what would have happened to him had we not invited him to become manager when we did. He wouldn't have gone out of the game because he had far too much to offer for that to have happened. But in Scotland he wasn't a target for Rangers or Celtic and we were really the only club he could have led into the big time because of the direction we had identified.

'Perhaps he would have gone to England, managed a club in the lower divisions and attracted attention – I firmly believe he would have got to the top sooner or later. But you can never be absolutely sure what would have happened and it is a source of immense satisfaction for us that we identified Fergie as a catalyst for our club and that he chose us, too.

'And what a time he gave us and this club gave him. You look back on it now and it worked so well on so many levels that, really, there are dream-like aspects to it. Who would have thought that we would get into a position where Rangers would ask us for our manager and that he would turn them down because they weren't right for him after what he had experienced here? Or that English clubs – big clubs like Wolves and Arsenal – would ask him to go down and look at what they had to offer and that he would see that it would be a step back for him?

'When Manchester United recognised what he had achieved here and what he could achieve for them, the time was right for him to move. He had become hungry for a new challenge and in many ways their situation resembled ours when Fergie came to Pittodrie. They had existed for years without winning the League but it was obvious that they should be accomplishing more than that. Alex Ferguson only had to sniff that promise in the air at Old Trafford and he realised he was the man who could do something to change it.'

Eric Black

Development manager at Celtic. Played for Aberdeen and Metz.

Eric Black joined Aberdeen at the age of 16 in 1980, two years after Alex Ferguson had been appointed manager and at a stage where the revolution being wrought at Pittodrie had been confirmed by a first Scottish championship. Although only 5ft 8in tall, Black became a prolific scorer in his time at Pittodrie before moving on to Metz in France. Ferguson subsequently declared that some of the younger players who had come through at Pittodrie when Aberdeen were enjoying unprecedented success became victims of burn-out, having been asked to perform in too many pressurised matches at too tender an age, and he cited Black as an example.

'I had been signed at 14 on a schoolboy form and went to Pittodrie for a couple of trials. My feelings were of awe and apprehension whenever Fergie was about because he had a reputation as a fiery and intimidating personality, but to his credit he was not a fearsome figure, at least as far as he dealt with the young lads. Although we were at the very bottom of the ladder he would come along and watch us in training regularly and I think he went out of his way to look at us and see how we were coming along.

'At that age it is easy to feel ignored at a club or that the manager is only interested in the older players, but Fergie's philosophy was that if we felt looked after and believed we were also part of a big club then we would be encouraged to do more. There was a change in attitude when I went full time and a certain fear factor came into play.

'If he wasn't happy with your performance he would certainly be critical and sometimes scathing. I didn't enjoy it at all but now that I work with young players myself I can relate to his methods. It can be very painful to be criticised in front of other people and we would sometimes get angry at it but, of course, nobody would ever say it to his face. I certainly would not have argued back even if I disagreed with something he might be saying. But you have to say his methods worked.

'When you knew he would tear you to shreds for a careless performance you did everything you could to make sure you avoided being a target which, of course, meant that he was getting through to us the message about concentrating all the time. His most important traits are a will to win and ruthlessness in dealing with anything or anybody who might get in the way. Mind you, there were times that his temper and anger were an act.

'I sometimes saw him two minutes before he was to go into the dressing room and he would be fine, chatting with people and telling jokes. Then he would turn around, walk into the dressing room and blast somebody to the end of the earth. The trouble was, as a player you couldn't be sure exactly when there was a bit of acting involved or when he was deadly serious so again it was an example of how he could keep people on their toes.

'Tactically, he has the gift of seeing problems or advantages in a game very quickly and he knows how to change it right away. In training he kept himself back and he used to leave most of it to Archie Knox. Archie would be hands-on and take control so that Fergie was able to stand back, which in coaching is perfect because if you become too involved you don't see the overall picture, the reaction of the players, whether they're really listening to you.

'People have said that I burned myself out at Pittodrie but if you asked me to do it again I would jump at it. It was a case of cup finals, championships and big European games one after another so what player is going to say no to that? How many Scottish players in recent years have wished they had to cope with that sort of pressure?

'I had an enjoyable playing career but now that I'm in coaching myself I look back on different managers I played under and I take something from each of them. What I got from Fergie was the need to demand high standards, especially nowadays when you have young players earning big money – far beyond anything we were getting at their age. It's easy for them to think they don't have to listen to what you say, that they can always move on and have another payday with another club.

'The Bosman judgment made it harder for managers to manage in the old-fashioned ways. I've heard that Fergie has changed, that he's not doing the complete shouting and bawling routine. Of course, you don't need to do so much of that when your team is going well because if the side is picking itself, which is more or less what happened with Aberdeen, then confidence is going to be good and the atmosphere is conducive to winning. Not that Fergie ever stopped having some way to give us an extra edge.

'He would tell us that such and such a journalist had written this about us in a newspaper and then just before we had a game we would see the cutting pinned up in the dressing room. Or he would have his rants about the bias towards the west of Scotland in the press and say sarcastically that the number-one reporters were up from Glasgow so we had better try to play well that day. He used whatever worked.

'We are far from being good friends. Put it this way, we're not on each other's Christmas card lists. He's a very contradictory character. You'll find him taking his teams along to old folks' homes or children's hospitals and there are times when he does that very quietly because he certainly doesn't forget his roots.

'Some players will think of him as a complete so-and-so but others will regard him as the Messiah. He wasn't the kind who had favourites openly but he's smart enough to keep himself onside with his more important players. It's all politics in football, no question. If he hadn't been a football manager I can just see Fergie as a shop steward.'

Craig Brown

Scotland manager. Former assistant Scotland manager.
Manager Clyde. Played for Rangers, Dundee and Falkirk.

'I first encountered Alex Ferguson in a schoolboy trial match, Glasgow v. West of Scotland, when we were on opposite sides. The following year we played together in the Scottish Schoolboys team which played England at Dulwich Hamlet and lost 4–3. I was the captain and I scored with a penalty kick but I don't seem to remember Fergie scoring – I have a nice photo of that team with the two of us in it.

'He hasn't changed in all these years. He was always – what shall we say? – fiery, bright, lively and aggressive, but I think the best word to describe him is probably "engaging". He's got a compelling personality. You can't help but like him or hate him. He's got a warmth about him which I think is very much to do with him being a Glaswegian. He's got the Glasgow patter, that's for sure, but he digs in. He was the union representative at most of the clubs he was at and he was quite a militant. I remember him threatening a strike when he was at Falkirk and he wouldn't have thought twice about calling it.

'He's got a cheeky, opportunist side to him which can be very amusing or very aggravating depending on whether you're with him or against him when it happens. When I played at Falkirk he had moved on to Dunfermline and we came up against each other in one game. I remember our goalkeeper, Willie Wigham, getting a pass back from another player, Willie Fulton.

'Willie Wigham wasn't too happy with the pass and he stood there with the ball in below his hand, swearing at Willie Fulton, telling him that he should have booted the ball up the park. Fergie strolled up and kicked the ball from below his hand into the net. Willie Wigham couldn't believe it and he went daft, but the referee was a Scottish legend, Tiny Wharton, a giant, imposing figure, and he allowed the goal.

'We had Fergie sauntering about very pleased with himself and Willie Wigham going crazy and we ended up on the wrong end of a bad defeat. So I've seen him operate as a schoolboy, a youth, a senior player and a manager over the years, but anything I can remember he would be able to add to because he has a phenomenal memory. It's actually unbelievable at times. He'll remember every player in the youth team and details about them that they've probably forgotten themselves.

'He'll say to me, "D'ye mind we played with Sandy Turpie and Jim Cruickshank was in goal?" And I'll be saying, "Aye, you're right – I couldn't have told you that." His photographic memory is one of his great attributes and when I worked with him in Mexico at the World Cup finals I discovered that at half-time he could recollect every move, every pass in the first half. Never mind a video camera, he can recount exactly how the game went.

'And it's not just the game he's at he remembers. He'll say to a player, "Three years ago when you played against Everton you took the throw-in the same way you did today and we lost possession and they went up the field and scored a goal." And the player thinks for a second and says, "Oh, I'd forgotten that." But Fergie wouldn't have forgotten.

'He's got an encylopaedic memory for individuals and players and games. In Aberdeen his great strength was his signing policy. He signed only seven players for money in eight years – and not one for more than £100,000. The rest he brought through the youths and yet he was so successful there.

'So his great attributes are his eye for a player, knowledge of the game, retentive memory and a ruthless determination to win. He understands psychology and he knows how to assert himself. At Aberdeen he was once on his way back from training when a bunch of younger players overtook him in their white Mercedes, having a laugh about it.

'When he got to the ground he said, "Right, you lot – into my car." And he took them back to the training pitch and made them run back. Or so I was told – but I can believe it.

'His love for the game has always been there. Without meaning to be derogatory, I think it's important to remember that he wasn't highly gifted but he had a passion for football, good football, and he expects everybody else to share that. There are managers who like their teams to be the opposite of what they were as players. I can think of examples of managers in Scotland and England who were cowards when they were players but they tell their teams to get stuck right into the opposition.

'You say, "Why does he tell them to be so hard when he was such a feartie himself?" Fergie's different. He wants his teams to play well but he's got more credibility with his players when he does tell them to go out and battle.

'It was a great honour for me when I was a first division manager and he phoned me and asked me to go with him to Mexico. That was the old pals act in operation. Some people were surprised that he took the manager of a wee club like Clyde, me being part time as well. But he didn't hold that against me. He knew I had my reasons and I was very grateful for that. I like to think we've got on well over all the years.

'There's no side to him. He's never two-faced. He's right out with what he thinks. I was down seeing him a few weeks ago and when I was in his office at the Cliff he said to me, "Look at that, Broon!" There was a picture on the wall of the 1992 Manchester United youth team – nine of them full internationalists. That's unbelievable. With Scotland we can pick the best youths from all the clubs for our youth team and not get nine full internationalists out of them.

'He's absolutely the best British manager of his generation. I think we have to say that Bob Paisley is the man to beat if we go back a few years because his record was thirteen trophies, including three European Cups. Brian Clough will be up there, too, because he won two European Cups with Nottingham Forest, a provincial outfit.

'Jock Stein won nine championships in Scotland plus the European Cup. Fergie has won five championships in England, which is comparable with nine in Scotland, and he won two European trophies, one in Scotland and one in England. I'm biased but I think Fergie is the best Scottish manager ever. That's high praise indeed.'

Teddy Scott

Kit manager, Aberdeen

Teddy Scott is part of the fabric at Pittodrie, where he has worked for more years than he cares to admit or anyone else can remember. Officially he is Aberdeen's kit manager but it is difficult to believe that the club would be able to function without him. The most common cry around the ground whenever some unexpected problem arises is: 'Where's Teddy? He'll fix it.' But what has earned him the respect of a succession of managers is his deep knowledge of the game and of players and his insights were praised by Alex Ferguson in his autobiographical account, *A Light in the North*.

'The first time I ever encountered Alex Ferguson was at a reserve game here at Pittodrie when he was playing with Falkirk. I had our players together and I was doing my team talk when suddenly the dressing-room door was flung wide open and this fellow breezed in and shouted to Des Herron, who was one of our lads: "Hi, Des! How're you doing?" And the rest of us just watched amazed while he had a chat with Des and then off he went back to his own dressing room.

'I said: "Who was that?" Des said: "Oh, that's Alex Ferguson. He's a pal of mine." Des was a great joker. He never stopped telling funny stories and the word was that he and Fergie and Billy Connolly hung about together and that they gave Billy some of his jokes. Anyway, I certainly didn't think Fergie was going to be my boss one day but when he did come here as manager we seemed to hit it off right away.

'He seems to know whether he's going to get on with people or not pretty quickly. I think I was very useful to him because I knew all the training routines and the training sites and I could tell him a bit about the players. One of the first things he did when he came here was to insist that he got all the newspapers delivered to him every morning. He would come in at 8.30 and he would go through them one by one very carefully. I read recently that Brian Kidd went into his office to tell him something and walked out again saying, "You're not listening to me!" because Fergie was so engrossed in the papers, so maybe nothing has changed.

'He wanted every scrap of information he could use and he wanted to know what everybody was saying about his team. If he saw something he didn't like he would say, "I'll get on to him and sort him out." I used to say to him sometimes, "Steady on, don't go tearing in," because he could be a wee bit impetuous.

'That's a side of him which most people probably think is typical but what would surprise folk who don't know him is that he has got an extremely kind heart. We used to employ a lot of OAPs to do wee odd jobs around the stadium – clean the seats, that sort of thing. They were old men who loved football and who were thrilled just to have something to do around the club and the ground. They would be having their cups of tea early in the morning and Fergie would always go in to see them and have a chat.

'He would never walk past them in a corridor without speaking to them, either. Do you know, he bought every one of them a bottle of whisky at Christmas? They loved him, just loved him, but it got out of hand because he and Archie Knox used to play a game called "tips" in the gym, the pair of them trying to score goals against each other. It was competitive, to say the least. They nearly came to blows a few times.

'So what did Fergie do? He went to the OAPs and said, "You'll need to come into the gym and support me." He got them in there but they didn't want to cheer when Fergie scored because they were scared of Archie who'd be stamping around in a temper. Then Archie got the S-form boys and the youths in to support him and they were all scared because Fergie would get worked up if Archie scored.

'Fergie really did care about the people he dealt with at the club. The hardest part of management for him was to tell a young lad that he didn't really fit the bill. We had a reserve game at Dunfermline once and Ian Ferguson, who went on to play for Rangers and Scotland, was up for a trial with us. Fergie and Archie thought he was too wee and wouldn't grow, so we didn't sign him.

'But Fergie got a hold of Craig Brown, who was the manager of Clyde at the time, and said, "Look, I think there might be a lad who could do you a turn." We went down to Glasgow to play Clyde a while later and I saw this youngster chatting to one of our players. The lad said, "You don't recognise me, do you?" It was Ian Ferguson, who had filled out and grown up.

'Craig sold him to St Mirren and he scored the winning goal for them in the Scottish Cup final against Dundee United. Then he went to Rangers for £1 million and played for Scotland, but it was Fergie who got him his start. Fergie was very fatherly with the young lads here. He looked after them as if they were his own. Before we sent any of them to digs in Aberdeen Fergie would go and inspect the place.

'Then at Christmas he would give the landlady a big box of chocolates or a bottle of whisky to make them feel appreciated. All of that stopped a long time ago. This is part of Fergie's secret, his attention to little details most other people wouldn't notice.

'I don't know whether he went in for memory training but he has an amazing ability to store information in his head. I've seen staff at the ground take calls for Fergie and say to him, "So and so called – I'll write down his number for you." And Fergie would say, "Don't bother. Just tell me the number and I won't forget it." Sure enough, he would pick up the phone an hour or two later and dial from memory.

'Because he hoards information he's always impressed when he sees other people doing the same. When Fergie came to us from St Mirren he brought a young player called Steve Cowan with him. Stevie worshipped Fergie. He would have run in front of a bus if Fergie had told him to do it. One day Fergie got all of the first team squad together for a team talk and when he went into the room he saw Steve Cowan sitting there.

'Fergie said, "What are you doing in here? You're no' in the squad." Stevie said, "Well, I just want to know everything that's going on." So Fergie let him stay because he admired Stevie's attitude. If players give him that kind of enthusiasm he's hugely protective of them. He'll defend any of them if the press have a go and the players respond to him because they know they can trust him.

'With his deep knowledge of the game and his love for it, as well as his ability to handle people and understand them, he is the greatest football manager I have ever encountered, without question.'

Dave Smith

Scotland's Player of the Year in 1972. Sweeper in Rangers side that won the Cup Winners' Cup that year. Subsequently player–coach Arbroath and Berwick Rangers. Played for Los Angeles Aztecs and in South Africa.

'I was signed in August 1966 from Aberdeen and Alec Smith – who was no relation – was bought from Dunfermline a couple of days before me. At that time Dunfermline were doing well in Europe because Jock Stein had been their manager until the season before and he had set them up as a good side, so Alec and I used to go through and watch them when we weren't playing.

'Fergie was playing for them at that time and he was scoring nearly all the time – 66 goals in 88 league games in the team which missed winning the 1964–5 championship by a single point – so if you watched Dunfermline you couldn't miss him. We knew what his style of play was – all elbows. Our manager, Scot Symon, had bought Alex from Dunfermline and he needed a striker who could do a good job for him because he was under pressure after Rangers lost to Berwick Rangers in the Scottish Cup in 1967, which was their worst ever defeat.

'The forwards up to that game had been Jim Forrest and George McLean but after Berwick they never played again. The thing was that although Rangers had been knocked out of the Scottish Cup by a wee team from the second division they were doing well in the Cup Winners' Cup and they got to the final in Nuremburg against Bayern Munich.

'They tried quite a few players at centre forward – Roger Hynd, Alec Smith and Sandy Jardine – but not one was a natural striker. When the team lost in extra time to Bayern Munich the chairman, John Lawrence, slaughtered them in the press, saying we had tried to win a European final with five half-backs in the forward positions.

'So Scot Symon, who was a good manager and respected by the players, was under pressure. He bought Fergie at the start of the

1967–8 season and he settled in well – he was our top scorer in his first season – but we had a couple of bad results home and away in Europe against Gornik from Poland and they sacked Symon the day after the second leg, even though we were actually top of the league over Jock Stein's Celtic.

'The new man was Davie White, Scot's assistant, but Davie didn't have much experience of handling big players because he had come from Clyde. And Fergie always spoke up for himself, so it might have been that Davie just didn't take to him in the first place. At the end of that season I remember we went on a trip to Denmark to wind down and we were invited to a reception at the British ambassador's residence.

'We all had to be introduced one by one to the ambassador by John Lawrence. The chairman was fine and he got everybody's name right until he came to Fergie, who was nearly the last in line. Lawrence said, "This is ... um ... this is ... oh, I just can't remember."

'It was very embarrassing and Fergie was furious but that wasn't the end of it. Later on we were all standing around holding drinks when we heard the ambassador say to the chairman, "Now, what's this I hear about you getting a new centre forward?" And the player they were talking about turned out to be Colin Stein of Hibs. Rangers paid £100,000 for him, which was a Scottish record transfer fee, and he scored hat tricks in his first two games.

'He was preferred to Fergie for most of the 1968–9 season, although it was Fergie who played in the Scottish Cup final against Celtic when we lost 4–0 and that really finished his career at Ibrox. But to get back to the trip to Denmark, it was a bad time for Fergie. He didn't get on at all well with Willie Allison, who was the Rangers historian and popular with the directors. Once we'd had a few drinks and came back to the hotel and Fergie was ranting about Willie Allison in a corridor but he didn't know that Willie was standing behind a door listening to everything he had to say, which I imagine got straight back to the board.

'Then there was a problem at training. We used to go to the Tivoli Gardens every day – Davie White came, too – and to give Fergie his due, he would have a few beers, go to his bed and start again with the best of them a few hours later. I've always thought that was why he was strict with his own players – he had written the dodge book himself and knew exactly what they could get up to.

'Anyway, on this occasion we really went at it one night, which might have been the evening Fergie had done all his washing and his shirts and socks and everything were steeping in the bath. When he came back he found that some of the others had tipped their ashtrays and any muck they could find into the bath. His clothes were filthy. None of this was behind the back of the manager because Davie White had been with us and he had been putting the beers away as well.

'But the next day at training Davie wanted us to do some exercise which involved heading the ball. Fergie had a terrible hangover and every time he headed the ball you could see it really hurt him. Mostly he was missing by five feet because he was probably seeing two balls and trying to head the wrong one, but again this was noted by the directors who were standing at the side of the pitch.

'It all came to a head at the end of the next season when we played Celtic in the Scottish Cup final at Hampden Park and lost 4–0. It was a very bad defeat and it started with Billy McNeill heading the opening goal after only two minutes. Alex had been told to mark Billy and he didn't, so it was a free header. There were fingers pointed on the pitch and there was a row in the dressing room later but it was probably unfair to heap the blame on Fergie. He wasn't that great a header of the ball, nor was he particularly big, and it would have taken something special to stop Billy McNeill, who could come in like a train. Plus the fact that our full-back, Kai Johansson, should have been on the post and he wasn't, so Billy could put the ball just where he wanted it.

'Fergie stood his ground but they had to have somebody to blame. And Fergie had rubbed them up the wrong way on other occasions so he was landed with it and they got rid of him to Falkirk. I don't think he's been all that fond of Rangers since then.'

CONTEMPORARIES

John Barnes

Double winner of Footballer of the Year. England international (78 caps). Captained Liverpool. Also played for Watford, Newcastle and Charlton.

There hasn't been much of an affinity between Liverpool and Manchester United for a number of reasons, but for John Barnes, synonymous with his success at Anfield, there is no animosity towards Alex Ferguson or resentment of his achievements.

Barnes says: 'When you talk about dynasties in football, there was clearly one built at Liverpool and one was under way from Sir Matt's time at Old Trafford. But the real dynasty at Manchester United has been under construction since Alex Ferguson came along. To create something that will last, it cannot materialise overnight. Alex Ferguson was given that opportunity to develop a dynasty and, although Arsenal have now won the league and apart from Liverpool where I believe a formidable team can arise again, I still think that Manchester United will be one of the powerful forces in Europe for many years to come.'

Barnes is one of the ITV 'team' of experts alongside Ferguson. He says: 'I have worked with Alex now and discovered that people's perceptions of him are wrong. He is actually a very easy-going kind of guy.

'You will see him leaving the ground and stopping to say hello to the crowd. He has time for everyone. He is a genuine person, even though he doesn't come across like that because of his image on TV.'

John Barnwell

Chief executive of the League Managers' Association.

John Barnwell gives an insight into Ferguson's droll humour. Barnwell, former Wolves manager, rang the Manchester United boss about the sixth annual dinner and presentations of the Association at Sopwell House Hotel, St Albans, in May 1998, where Arsene Wenger was Manager of the Year as Arsenal had just taken Manchester United's title.

Ferguson indicated he was attending, and Barnwell invited him to play in the golf tournament that preceded the dinner. Ferguson agreed, saying, 'I've got to win something this season.'

Ken Bates

Chelsea chairman. Chairman of Wembley National Stadium Ltd. and F.A. Councillor.

The Chelsea chairman has one of the most cosmopolitan teams and management structures in British football, but he still admires the down-to-earth qualities that he believes make Alex Ferguson's Manchester United team the one to beat.

He says: 'Alex Ferguson has my utmost admiration for his success and it's his great attention to detail that impresses me the most. To become the greatest British manager of all time there has been some fierce competition, with Bill Shankly and Bob Paisley, but he has probably surpassed both of them – and he is still there.

'Matt Busby was a fantastic manager. He had flair and style and did if "off the wall" in many respects. In comparison Ferguson is ruthlessly efficient, the most thorough professional in the game ever. I have never seen anybody in the game so dedicated, so professional, so thorough.

'He still has the team that everybody has to beat to win something.

'He has Roy Keane back for this season's campaign and I felt he was the key player that they missed all last season. Liverpool, too, are the club you have to finish above. I appreciate they haven't won anything for some time now but together with Manchester United they are the powerhouses of the North. In the South you cannot discount the new champions, Arsenal, and, of course, Chelsea, and long may that continue.'

It's mostly the people inside the game, those that Ferguson can relate to the best, who know the other side of his abrasive character. As Bates said: 'He has quite a sense of humour that is not obvious to a lot of people, and because of that we have our little banters from time to time. I love to get him going, and I can say something totally outrageous to him and he will burst out laughing rather than take offence.

'When we lost to Manchester United in the FA Cup semi-final at Villa Park, I bumped into him immediately after the game and said, "Who says crime doesn't pay?" At first there was a look of outrage and then he just burst out laughing.'

Bates has also heard a tale about Ferguson which only served to heighten his admiration for the man and the manager. Whether fact or myth, Bates enjoys recounting the story. 'I have heard that when Alex Ferguson took over at Aberdeen one of his first tasks was to call together all of his scouts. So the story goes, he told them that he didn't want to discover that any kid who lived within a 30-mile radius of Pittodrie had signed for any other club, or he would beat the living daylights out of the scout responsible. The upshot was that he developed an exceedingly good youth team! Now, you've got to admire something like that. If it's true of course.'

Bobby Campbell

Former Arsenal and QPR coach. Former manager of Chelsea, Fulham and Portsmouth.

Bobby Campbell has an unusual accolade for Alex Ferguson – the best listener he has ever met.

He says: 'When I was manager of Fulham, we went to Scotland in the Anglo-Scottish Cup and Alex's side beat us by four goals. I went back to the hotel after the game and got a telephone call from him, asking me if we could meet as he did not have many opportunities to talk to anybody about English league football. He came to the hotel and we had a cup of tea and a chat. It was the first time I had met him. He said he never got a chance to talk to anyone from England.

'I was a relatively young manager myself in the 1970s, but we sat up half the night, talking about football and discussing the likes of my experiences with players like George Best, Rodney Marsh and Bobby Moore at Fulham. He was also interested to hear how I had introduced Liam Brady and David O'Leary to the Arsenal team and how I had dealt with the likes of Terry Venables and Gerry Francis when I was coach at QPR. Looking back at it, Alex listened and took note and used all I told him as experience as he shot up the ladder as a manager.'

Eric Cantona

Former French international. Multiple championship winner. FA Cup winner. Clubs include Auxerre, Marseille, Leeds and Manchester United.

Alex Ferguson bought Eric Cantona for a modest £1 million from Leeds, and over the next four and a half years nurtured a priceless gem that sparkled in the glow of six major silver trophies.

Cantona, as he contemplates a new life in the theatre and films, will always be indebted to Ferguson for believing in him during troubled times. When others called for his head and doubted the wisdom of allowing him to continue wearing the famous red strip, the United boss stood by his man.

And Cantona won't forget it.

He says: 'I am grateful to Alex Ferguson and proud that I belonged to a side that is compared to the great Manchester United teams of the past. The manager signed me in the first place knowing the risk he might have been taking if he had believed all the tales he had heard about me.

'He enjoyed himself in a magnificent career as a player and manager. Although when he advised me about the rights and wrongs of retaliation he let slip that he had been sent off more times than I had.

'He was the boss, though. A lover of football. Someone who would be watching boys playing in the rain if he did not happen to be manager of the biggest club in Britain. The only time when he didn't think about football was when he was on the bus to away games playing cards with the players.

'I am proud to belong and proud that we have honoured the names of George Best, Denis Law, Bobby Charlton and the great Sir Matt Busby by trying to follow in their great tradition. Alex was the head of my family. A man I will honour for all time.'

The two men had their fall-outs. Great minds don't always think alike, as they say. But at the end, when Cantona broke the sad news to the boss in his office, they parted with a firm handshake.

Ferguson never flinched from making the unpredictable Frenchman toe the line. He was bawled out in the same way as everyone else at Old Trafford.

The United boss says: 'Players get it between the eyeballs generally if it's criticism. But Eric knew that whatever happened it would be in the dressing room or in my office and that was the finish of it. I don't bear grudges. I don't have the time and it's not part of my management strategy.'

Ferguson fully believes that the loyalty they shared was the crucial factor behind the club's astonishing success in winning four titles and two FA Cups together.

There were those mad moments which threatened to wreck the partnership, but Ferguson stood strong in the belief that after the Crystal Palace bust-up Cantona would never let him down again.

He didn't, and the United boss adds: 'Eric knew that I don't desert my players. He knew he could always depend on me.'

Cantona was comforted by that trust and always knew that if they had to part it would be on his say-so. He says in his book *Cantona – My Story* that he had prepared himself for the day he would have to say goodbye to it all.

'The shape of my life shows that I am always on the move, whatever the club is, whatever the town is that welcomes me,' he wrote. 'I have suffered too much from becoming attached to things in the past. I've been hurt too many times to ever let myself feel that I belong. Whatever club I am at I never think of myself as a permanent fixture. It is important to have been places. I have travelled. I've seen many people and that's important for yourself and your relationship with others.

'But it is only at the moment when the door opens that one can know how much one is attached to a place, a house or to a family.

'I will never be motivated by money, though. It has not changed my life and never will. Stupid people are convinced that a footballer goes only where the money is. If they don't want to die as idiots they should know that there are other things which also form part of negotiations.

'At the end, though, I will survive. It is when you hit difficult moments in life and you come through that you can say to yourself: "Yes, I've other things besides my football talent."

'Life is always too cruel. I just say to myself that I am always passing through. Let's try to pass the ball and let the sun shine. Let's hope it shines on everyone...'

Sir Bobby Charlton

*Manchester United director. World Cup winning team 1966.
Record goalscorer for England – 49. Founder of soccer school.
Played for Manchester United.*

The most valid assessment of Alex Ferguson's career in management is delivered by none other than Sir Bobby himself. Subjective he might be, but from inside the Old Trafford boardroom it is clear that Ferguson is held in the highest esteem.

Sir Bobby says: 'Most people would say that if Alex Ferguson were to win the European Cup, he would go down as the greatest manager in Manchester United's history and this country's history. He has proved that his successful formula hasn't just worked with one team – he has built more than one team at this club. He has the personality and the ability to get the best out of players and his staff.

'One thing sets him aside from most of his contemporaries. He has achieved success consistently. In the modern game, managers can become casualties of even their own success because after three or four years they have to move on as their players don't seem to listen to them any more. But Alex is not afraid to take on that challenge. A mark of his success is that everybody wants to play for him. He has earned their respect. Even the youngsters want to come to Manchester United because they know the manager's philosophy is that if they are good enough then they will get a game irrespective of their age. He gives them hope and confidence. Confidence goes right through the club. He has created success at every level of the club and that all reflects in the glory years he has brought to it.

'From the moment he arrived to take charge of the team he has had this enthusiasm for the game. He is quite prepared to travel 300 miles, through the night if necessary, if he thinks there is a player he needs to watch before thinking about signing him, even if it is a young player.

He will jump in his car at any time to cover a match anywhere if he thinks it will be worthwhile, with one motive – to bring success to his team.'

Of course, there was no overnight success for Ferguson at Old Trafford. The club had to wait four years before the results of his methods kicked in. The Manchester United board had patience, although there was a great deal of speculation at the time that it was wearing thin and that they thought about a change of direction. Sir Bobby explains why they stuck with Ferguson. 'You can tell when something is right. You don't have to be a great soothsayer when you can see that someone can do a good job. Everybody would prefer success to come immediately, but it doesn't happen that way, and we could see the potential. We were quite certain he was the correct man for the job. What happened with Ferguson should be a good example to others. Too many clubs don't give their managers the backing they deserve. Sometimes the crowd prove to be too influential in calling for a manager to go.

'There were never any personality clashes here at Old Trafford between the board and the manager – we just knew we had the right man. When he arrived he said that to build the team he wanted it would take between three and four years. He would need to wait for contracts to expire to let players go and to acquire the ones he wanted. He has been proved right in that.'

Sir Bobby knows the workload Ferguson takes upon himself. He drives himself all over the country. But Sir Bobby doesn't relish being a passenger. He explains: 'When he used to live in Aberdeen and had to watch players he would be travelling hundreds of miles – he must have lived in his car. For someone who is such an experienced driver, I must say it's a nightmare to be a passenger in his car! He is so anxious to pass every car ahead of him that he gets right up close to the car in front. For Alex time is of the essence.'

Sir Bobby plays golf with Ferguson. 'I see a lot of him socially, mostly on the golf course. Quite frankly it's best if I don't say too much about his golf – it's pretty bad, really.'

Despite this, Sir Bobby Charlton is delighted when he can drag Alex Ferguson on to the golf course to cut short his normal 20-hour working day – a chance to get him to relax, unwind and recharge batteries after destroying another million or so brain cells in masterminding one more Double campaign.

But Sir Bobby knows he's fighting a losing battle. When he shouts

'Fore', Fergie will probably answer '*nil*'! When he talks of being bunkered, the Manchester United boss will automatically think of Kevin Keegan.

Ferguson just can't relax even when he's away from the job of building United into a soccer dynasty designed to last long after the year 2000. It's his whole life and occupies every waking minute.

Sir Bobby just shakes his head when he says: 'Sometimes you can get him out to dinner or maybe on to the golf course. And, really, he's quite pleased when people sometimes give him the chance to step away from it a little. But it doesn't make much difference. All he wants to do is talk about United. His mind is never off it.

'Yet these demands are not from the club. He puts those demands on himself. Despite his heavy schedule I believe he will never ever experience what you might call burn-out. This is his life's work. It's what Alex Ferguson is all about. And I can see him just going on and on...'

Sir Bobby has admired the man since he exploded on to the Old Trafford scene on Bonfire Night in 1986. He was convinced that the former Aberdeen chief was the only man capable of lifting the club out of crisis following the failure of five previous managers to win the championship.

'He was desperate for the job – he couldn't wait,' added Charlton. 'Managing Manchester United was the ultimate challenge. There was no fear in him. No worry that having become such a big name in Scotland it would all go wrong down here.

'I had persuaded the club to talk to Alex and I'm proud of that. I've always believed he would crack it here. But the credit only goes to one person – Alex Ferguson.

'It was bound to take him time to get things moving in the way he wanted. But once he cracked it with his first trophy there was never going to be any stopping him. I always believed that.'

Sir Bobby's confidence wasn't even shaken by a rocky start that had many inside and outside Old Trafford calling for Ferguson's head. He looked likely to follow Wilf McGuinness, Frank O'Farrell, Tommy Docherty, Dave Sexton and Ron Atkinson down the same road to nowhere.

But his first triumph in the 1990 FA Cup saved his neck and started the golden ball rolling, with trophies dropping as regularly as lottery balls.

Sir Bobby adds: 'Personally I never had any doubts about what Alex could achieve with us. By the time we won at Wembley in 1990 I reckon he was bang on course. I knew people had been calling for his head but as a board of directors we decided that when we appointed Alex we were going to give him the time he needed no matter what.

'I believe we are on course to stay as England's dominant force way into the next century. And that's down to Alex. He has shown incredible self-belief, great personal resilience, tactical awareness – and just would not let himself be deflected.

'Now we are reaping the rewards of Alex's master plan, something that took quite some time to come together. We are setting the standard for others to follow. Everything is in place. We have shown the value of having faith in your manager. You have to be positive. We had the right man so we gave him the time he needed.

'Alex has helped lead a revolution at Old Trafford and he was given the backing to do it. He got down to business right away, sometimes working 20 hours a day. He still does that. There's no question of him relaxing and delegating responsibility. In fact, the only problem is calming him down, making him take a break. That is just about imposs-ible.'

Sir Bobby observes: 'He is an enthusiast, and he's always talking about the game. He knows every player at every club. He has earned his success.'

From within the boardroom Sir Bobby is sure that Ferguson will carry on. 'There's still a lot more for him to achieve. He has never really talked about retirement. It is reasonable to talk about retirement when you're feeling a bit tired, and maybe he has felt that way at times, but I can still see him keeping going.

'We all want him to win the European Cup and fulfil all of our dreams – the directors' and the fans'. He's given us exciting times and an exciting team, and that's precisely what we wanted at Manchester United – let's hope it continues.'

David Dein

Arsenal vice-chairman. FA counsellor. Representative on UEFA.

It would be understandable for the Arsenal camp to have a less than favourable opinion of Ferguson. Not at all. From the highest level within the boardroom there is nothing but admiration. Yet there have been numerous high-profile clashes which have left the two clubs seemingly at endless loggerheads – from Arsene Wenger's so-called mind games with the Old Trafford boss to the ugly 'racial' confrontation between Peter Schmeichel and Ian Wright in recent times to conflicts that go back to the time both clubs were docked points for an on-pitch brawl.

But David Dein enthuses about Fergie's talents for which he has the highest regard. 'His success stands for all to see; it is a testament to his ability as a manager. I am a great admirer of Alex and what he has achieved at Manchester United. The club went through a long barren patch before his arrival, and though it took a few years before he won his first trophy he then delivered the title for the first time in around a quarter of a century.'

In fact, Dein considered recruiting Ferguson before Arsenal appointed one of their old boys, George Graham, to the managerial office at Highbury. Dein opens up the secrets of the Highbury boardroom to reveal how he considered Ferguson as one of the Gunners' managerial candidates to take over from Don Howe.

He recalls: 'Yes, we nearly employed Alex. I met him a couple of times in Aberdeen before he went to Manchester United. I had a number of meetings with him and he was seriously considered for our position, but in the end we decided to go for an ex-Arsenal man in George Graham. We took George from Millwall even though he was relatively untried. We didn't offer the managerial post to Alex Ferguson.

'I have met Alex more than a dozen times over the years and I have always found him to be an extremely astute man.'

Above left It could be any one of Manchester United's clean cut-starlets, but it's Ferguson in his playing days.
Above right The pleasure at having made the dream move to Glasgow Rangers is evident.

Ferguson was always as uncompromising on the pitch as he would later prove to be on the touchline and in the boardroom.

Left Arsenal's Terry Neill tries in vain to get the ball off Ferguson in a typically passionate Anglo-Scottish clash.

Below Ferguson breaks, at least temporarily, the Rangers-Celtic stranglehold on Scottish football.

A rare moment with his feet up early in his career as a manager.

Above left Perfecting the managerial wave from an open top bus as he brings home the silverware for Aberdeen. It is a skill he will have plenty of opportunities to exercise in the coming years.

Above right A brief reign as Scotland manager and another brief spell in the sun for the national team.

A first taste of European glory.

The dream team.

Above The love affair with the Premiership trophy.

Left Never one to keep his opinions to himself Ferguson remonstrates with the officials during a match against Blackburn Rovers.

Above left Ferguson is no less vociferous with his own players.
Above right Celebrating the extraordinary end to the 95–96 season with one of his most popular players, Eric Cantona.

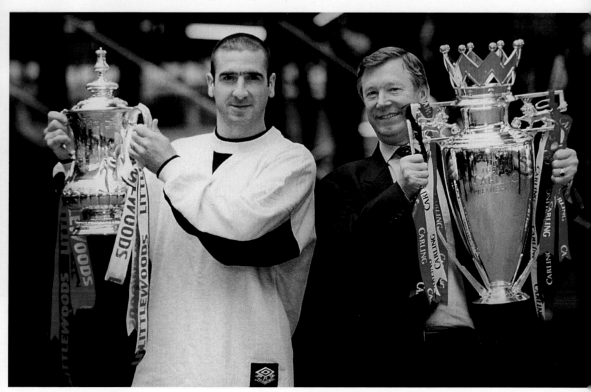

The Auld Alliance comes good as Ferguson and Cantona revel in the double.

Above left In the frame with another legend, Sir Matt Busby; this time posing with the European Cup.
Above right In company with Sir Bobby Charlton, and slightly the worse for wear, as a FA Cup celebration begins to take its toll.

The shirt hasn't always fitted Andy Cole but Ferguson has found a winning formula with Cole often enough to make his record £7million signing fee pay.

Catch them young.

Above left Alex Ferguson must be wondering how he would cope if he ever won the treble.
Above right Racking up yet another award for managerial prowess.

Honours from the Queen. Simply the best.

Tommy Docherty

Preceded Alex Ferguson as Manchester United manager.

The Doc was sacked from Old Trafford for private reasons after winning the FA Cup, and following the reigns of Dave Sexton and Ron Atkinson came the Alex Ferguson regime. Once one of Ferguson's old friends, the Doc has since fallen out with him, following Leeds United's championship win in 1991–2.

Tommy Docherty, now an after-dinner speaker, radio and TV pundit, recalls that he felt that Manchester United lost that title rather than Leeds winning it because Ferguson 'chopped and changed the team' in the run-in.

That criticism never went down very well with Ferguson. In fact, they've never spoken since. The main reason for the fall-out was that Docherty went public and said that Fergie reminded him of an arsonist, adding: 'But even an arsonist wouldn't throw away his last three matches!' It was a typical Tommy Doc quip, but Ferguson never saw the funny side of that one.

Despite the fall-out, Docherty fully acknowledges Ferguson's place among the all-time great managers.

Paul Durkin

FIFA World Cup referee.

Alex Ferguson is no different to most managers. They've had words about referees, Ferguson probably more than most. He would not be high on the referees' list of guest speakers at their annual bash.

Paul Durkin recalls a moment when even Ferguson was in a good mood with the officials. He knows because he was in charge of the game when Manchester United won the championship at the Riverside Stadium.

He recalls: 'Alex personally brought a bottle of champagne for the officials. He said everybody else was having some so why not us? He came into our room and simply said, "Thanks very much." No doubt he was happy because they had won 3–0 and won the League!

'Other than that, I've had little to nothing to do with him. I don't know the guy. Usually the managers bring the team sheets to the referee half an hour before kick-off, but Ferguson left that to Brian Kidd so I don't really have a lot of contact with him – unless he talks to everyone else but not to me!

'Let's be honest about it – the only time a manager wants to speak to a referee is when he wants to moan and groan! However, he's not had too much to moan about to me – Manchester United have only lost once when I've been in charge! Although that was against Arsenal a couple of years ago.'

Doug Ellis

Aston Villa chairman.

Doug Ellis enjoys recounting the tale of Alex Ferguson and the cross-border transfer tribunal over the signing of Neil Cooper for Aston Villa from Aberdeen.

The Villa manager of the time was Graham Turner and Ferguson and his Aberdeen chairman and his son were present at the tribunal as Ellis takes up the story.

'The four-man panel of judges all came from Ireland and the usual procedure in these tribunals, which I might add I've chaired several times, is that the buying club makes its representations followed by the other club. Each party makes their points separately and then they both go before the panel to be told the price and the conditions of sale, and there is no form of appeal. Once we had both made our cases, we were in the corridor together outside the tribunal room. I turned to Alex and his chairman and said, "Look, we're in the hands of these people ... we are in football together, so whatever their decision we won't dispute it, argue about it or have any animosity toward each other about it."

'They nodded in agreement and we all shook hands on what was a gentlemanly way of going about a difficult situation for everyone. Then we were all called in to hear the verdict. The price was set at £500,000. At just half a million for Neil Cooper we were absolutely delighted. Alex went mad, raving mad, absolutely potty; he went red in the face and started shouting and bawling. The deputy chairman was tapping him on the knee under the table and urging him to calm down and keep quiet and said to him, "Remember what we had agreed."

'Alex got up to storm out. I got up to stop him and offer him my hand. He refused to shake it. But I am sure he has matured since then!

And before anyone gets the wrong impression, we have been great friends since then, even though there are times when I cannot understand a word he says – and that's saying something, considering I had Tommy Docherty as one of my managers.'

Doug relates the anecdote with great relish but without any hint of bitterness – quite the reverse. He has the utmost admiration for Ferguson, although as one of the games longest-serving chairmen he doesn't join those queuing up to bestow the title of best manager of all time on Ferguson.

He explains: 'Alex is a winner and has done exceptionally well – no one can argue against that. But if you are assessing the best British managers then I go back an awful long way. I'm an old man with a long, long memory. Shankly, Bill Nicholson and Stan Cullis come to mind. There is, of course, only one Shanks, and Stan Cullis did a great job for Wolves. Certainly in the current decade Alex Ferguson is the No. 1, and we don't really know enough of Arsene Wenger quite yet, although I can tell you that the Arsenal manager fears Chelsea more than he does Manchester United. Maybe it's because they are just down the road or maybe it's because they have so many foreign players.

'The other problem area in assessing the manager of Manchester United is that you could manage that club the way it is at the moment. Certainly Alex's position was in jeopardy at one stage and he has turned it all around. There's an old saying in football that when the team is successful the manager gets all the praise but when it fails the chairman takes all the bullets.'

Equally, when the team fails the manager can get the bullet! Manchester United stuck with Ferguson and have now got their reward. Ellis adds: 'Perhaps if he didn't have the financial clout a club like Manchester United can give him, from a chairman like Martin Edwards, he might not be quite the same.'

Edward Freedman

Former marketing chief at Old Trafford. Head of Zone publishing, he originated the official Manchester United magazine.

Edward Freedman was responsible for transforming Manchester United into a marketing money machine with their merchandising and megastores.

Old Trafford is now a public company with a Stock Exchange listing that is the envy of the rest of the world, let alone the Premiership. In 1998 the company posted half-year profits before tax of £14.8 million, down from £19.4 million, mainly because of a big increase in transfer spending, including Teddy Sheringham's £3.5 million move from Tottenham the previous summer. Turnover, though, was up from £50.1 million to £51.6 million. At the same stage the year before, the club was showing a £3.7 million profit on transfers, but the latest figures revealed a £2.6 million deficit.

Underlying profits, before transfer fees, increased from £15.7 million to £17.5 million, and shareholders will receive a half-year dividend of 0.52p, up from 0.40p. Gate receipts rose by £600,000 to £19 million, reflecting average attendances of 54,800, against an average of 54,100 and an increase in prices and the introduction of a thousand new executive seats. Conference and catering incomes were boosted by 17% to £3.6 million, thanks to greater use of the stadium on non-match days.

Television income rose from £5.9 million to £7.9 million on the back of the new Premier League contract with BSkyB and the club's participation in the Champions' League.

Sponsorship income, which also included the Umbro kit deal, rose by £300,000 to £5.5 million. Merchandising turnover fell by 11% to £15.6 million because of a decrease in replica home kit sales. A new revolutionary zip-up strip would change that. United agreed a new two-year shirt sponsorship deal with existing backers Sharp – the most lucrative in Britain.

The club's new museum was officially opened by Pele on 11 April 1998. United have also received outline planning permission for a new £14.3 million training complex at Carrington. The club launched their own TV channel, MUTV, in partnership with BSkyB and Granada, and now, of course, there is the Murdoch takeover bid valuing the club at £623.4 million.

How much of this cash mountain is down to Alex Ferguson and the Manchester United success story on the pitch?

Freedman says: 'It's extremely hard to quantify but I would estimate that Alex Ferguson's success and having a winning team accounts for between ten per cent and twenty per cent of the company's profits. That's how I would look upon it. There is no question – a winning team helps enormously but you have to have an infrastructure in place to cash in on all that success.'

Because Ferguson and his team were fundamental to building the marketing and commercial Old Trafford empire, Freedman campaigned for more recognition and participation for the manager within the boardroom. He revealed: 'I don't think Alex participated nearly enough. He should have been involved sitting in on the board meetings and been part of the discussions about the developments at the club. Despite my arguments, the chairman wasn't entirely convinced and it didn't happen.'

Freedman consulted Ferguson on the general content of the official club magazine he initiated, particularly concentrating on the contributions from the star players. Ferguson has been very protective about his young players being exposed prematurely to the media. David Beckham was a prime example. But he allowed them access to the public via the magazine, albeit with careful handling and guidance.

Freedman says: 'I found Alex to be straightforward and very co-operative. If I ever had a problem with him he would come to me and confront me with it directly. There was no going behind my back.' Freedman joined Manchester United after building up the marketing and merchandising side of the PLC operation at Spurs under chairman Irving Scholar. Freedman observed: 'I would say that Alex Ferguson was different to deal with than, say, Terry Venables.'

He enjoyed a number of relaxed nights out in Ferguson's company.

He said: 'Alex was at his best during a relaxed social evening. He comes across as sincere and genuine. He asks your opinion about football and actually listens to what you have got to say – that makes a change in this game. It was never like that with someone like Terry Venables – he was always very secretive about what was in his head. Alex, in contrast, was very, very open and willing to discuss his views on football with those he trusted. In fact, he is a very sociable person, good fun, good company. Nothing like his image.'

Ruud Gullit

Former Dutch international. Ex-Chelsea player–manager.
Former World No. 1 footballer. European Footballer of the Year.
European Cup winner with AC Milan. Clubs – PSV Eindhoven,
AC Milan, Sampdoria, Chelsea. Newcastle United Manager.

Alex Ferguson's joy at pulling off a draw at Stamford Bridge on the way to his last title illustrated the suspicion within Old Trafford that Chelsea under Ruud Gullit were an emerging force to be respected.

At the time of Gullit's shock dismissal Chelsea were second in the Premiership, still involved in the Coca-Cola Cup and the quarter-finals of the Cup Winners' Cup, but the holders of the FA Cup had been eliminated in an awesome performance by Manchester United in the third round at the Bridge.

While Gullit was sacked, ostensibly over a pay row, United looked back at that 5–3 FA Cup triumph as the turning point of their season. They never again reached such heights and ended the season empty-handed while Chelsea, under the new management of Luca Vialli, clinched a cup Double with the foundations of the Gullit team.

Ferguson was in contact with Gullit virtually immediately he returned from his scouting abroad and their mutual respect has been un-diminished by events. Ironically, Chelsea chairman Ken Bates compared the Ferguson work ethic to the new Continental approach by Gullit as one of the prime reasons for the Dutchman's dismissal.

Gullit, speaking before his appointment to the Newcastle job changed everything, said: 'He asked me to join him at the club's training ground whenever I wanted to. I saw him again at the World Cup and he told me he still wanted me to watch his team train. Maybe I will do that when I am back in England. It was an extremely nice request from him.

'We have respect for each other as managers and coaches. Its okay to be enemies on the pitch, but we can respect each other's work.'

That mutual respect first came to light when Ferguson admitted, in the Old Trafford match-day programme notes, that his big regret is not signing Gullit as a player. Gullit says: 'Yes, I remember that, and once again that shows that we have a lot of respect for each other.'

Gullit talks about his admiration for Ferguson's managerial qualities. 'He is very strict. He knows exactly what he wants and most importantly he knows how to transmit this to his players. This is perhaps his best quality.' Ferguson might be a superb communicator with his players but Gullit laughs loudly when he adds: 'The problem is that I cannot understand him all the time – it's that accent!'

Gullit enjoys Ferguson's company. 'He is very comfortable, he is very funny. He talks a lot and I like to listen to him talk. He tells some wonderful stories about the game, and it is nice to hear someone of such vast experience imparting such knowledge.'

The universal acceptance that Ferguson is one of the best, if not the best, British bosses of all time doesn't sit uncomfortably with Gullit. He says: 'He has benefited from having the chance to be the coach of a club like Manchester United for a long time, and in an era when directors are not so patient and want immediate success. The club have not underestimated his abilities and understood those qualities and kept going with him until he brought the success they wanted. That is a lesson for many clubs to follow. Directors must have more patience ... Rome was not built in one day!'

He concludes, 'Bill Shankly at Liverpool is regarded as the best British manager, but Alex Ferguson now has a lot of experience and the most important thing is that he is still there and that he is still in charge of probably the best team in the country. He wants to prove again that they are the best team in English football.

'He has worked in a lot of places, and it has been tough for him, but that has made him the coach that he is.'

Sam Hammam

Part-owner, Wimbledon.

As owner of one of the game's humble little clubs for many years, Sam Hammam has learned the art of survival. Alex Ferguson and Manchester United are on a different planet in terms of support and investment in their team, yet the Dons remain in the Premiership, rubbing shoulders with their rich relations.

Hammam's admiration for Ferguson extends far beyond his achievements at Old Trafford, where success is expected as almost routine. Hammam explains: 'What makes Alex Ferguson so special, the most distinguished manager of his generation, is that not only has he been such a success at Manchester United – he would have also been successful had he been manager of Wimbledon or Doncaster or even Halifax.

'I have come to know him over the years. Whenever Manchester United come to London to play us, they stay overnight in a hotel and Alex arrives early to have a chat. We sit and talk for ages and I have come to recognise that he does not live in an ivory tower like some manager who represents one of the élite. Alex is not interested in after-dinner speaking, polishing his TV personality or opening shops. He is, though, one of the hardest workers in the game. He also knows everyone in his youth team, he's met their parents and has done his homework. That is his great strength. He has concentrated on the youth and reserve teams and hasn't had to just throw money at buying players. He takes an interest in every aspect of the club and knows about the finances. He knows the nitty-gritty of running a football club rather than being in cloud-cuckoo-land.

'Most managers would say, "Give me £10 million to buy the best player available." But running clubs at Wimbledon or Doncaster encompasses far more awareness than that. He is a detailer and a worker with knowledge deeply rooted about the workings of a football club rather than being a big-time Charlie.

'Anyone who had achieved as much success as Alex might be in danger of losing a few screws. Instead he has shown himself to be a man of steel; no screws lost.'

However, there are some who might suggest that Alex Ferguson can, at times, easily lose his marbles! Hammam has seen the red mist descend over Ferguson in one of the most infamous clashes in football – the so-called 'Tunnel of Hate' when Viv Anderson and John Fashanu had some pre-half-time discussions en route to the Plough Lane dressing rooms.

Hammam witnessed the violence. He recalls: 'We beat Manchester United 1–0 in the FA Cup that day and John Fashanu and Viv Anderson fought in the tunnel. Viv ended up needing treatment in the Manchester United dressing room, while John Fashanu was sitting in our dressing room.

'Alex Ferguson came tearing down the tunnel and he wanted to enter our dressing room to beat up John Fashanu. All the king's horses and all the king's men weren't going to stop him. That is, apart from Don Howe. Don was standing there in the middle of the narrow entrance with both arms spread out to reach either wall. Don was emphatic, "No, Alex, no, you're not going in there."

'There was no doubt, as far as I was concerned, that Alex was not simply going in there to give Fash a piece of his mind. He was ready to fight him. Alex is tough as nails, and very single-minded. He was furious. He was out to protect his own and I don't blame him for that. I am not going to reveal precisely what Alex was saying but, judging by his state of mind, he was ready to fight the whole damn troop, let alone Big Fash.

'We have talked about it since. He can laugh about it now.'

Kevin Keegan

Temporary England coach. Fulham chief operating officer. Ex-Newcastle United manager. Played for England, Liverpool, Hamburg, Southampton and Newcastle. Twice European Footballer of the Year.

An enduring TV image was that of Kevin Keegan visibly shaking with his headphones as he lambasted Alex Ferguson for his mind-game tactics in the run-in to the championship when Keegan's Newcastle blew up and Manchester United took the title. No love lost between two of the giants of the game.

Astonishingly, at least so it seemed, the two were hugging each other not too long afterwards – and again on television. In fact, especially for TV. ITV signed up Keegan to join Ferguson as part of their star-studded panel of experts.

Together again when ITV paraded their World Cup line-up at the Sports Café in London's Haymarket, with Keegan just missing out on the play-off finals with Fulham and Ferguson deposed by Arsene Wenger as the manager of the year with his team second to the Gunners, the acrimonious title clash between Ferguson and Keegan was well and truly consigned to history. Also on parade, along with Ruud Gullit, Terry Venables, John Barnes and Barry Venison, was Bobby Robson. Keegan joked: 'There's a manager who dropped me for England and another manager I'm supposed to hate. The fact is we all get on just great.

'I know what everybody thinks, but we have no problems. Yes, it was a battle for the championship and he probably said things he regrets and I certainly said things that I now regret. But Alex and I have a lot in common, funnily enough. It wasn't until I got to know him better that I discovered that Fergie is into horse racing. He has a horse called Queensland Star and I've got a couple of two-year-olds.'

Keegan was an admirer of Ferguson long before his huge success in

English football. He recalls: 'I first met Alex when Southampton were involved in a tournament with Aberdeen. At that time I didn't know who he was! The organisation of the tournament and the impact he had on that tournament showed you what football management was all about, and it's not all about just picking the right team. At Aberdeen he was in charge of virtually running the club.

'So it was really no surprise to me that he achieved so much when he moved from Aberdeen to Manchester United. He's a winner . . . even if he was a lucky winner when it came to beating Newcastle to the title!'

Graham Kelly

Former chief executive of the Football Association.

There can be no greater accolade for Alex Ferguson than the fact that he could have become the first Scottish manager to coach the England national team in the history of English football.

It is a matter of record that Ferguson revealed in his diary of the last championship season that an approach was made from within Lancaster Gate. However, the FA maintained a discreet and diplomatic silence during the inevitable headline-grabbing episode that clearly successfully publicised his book. Glenn Hoddle was still settling into the job and negotiating a hazardous World Cup qualifying route.

Hoddle eventually topped the tricky group ahead of Italy after that epic encounter in Rome and then took England to the Finals, returning with renewed hope for the future after utilising a number of Ferguson's outstanding youngsters.

There might have been a fire at Lancaster Gate which caused major disruption, but that was cool compared to the burning issue of whether, in fact, Ferguson was a realistic contender to ever become England boss.

Graham Kelly is one of only a handful of people who knew the truth. First the former FA's chief executive provided his personal view of Alex Ferguson's credentials and status within the game when he said: 'I think his record of success in the game puts him right up there at the top. Comparisons are always very difficult but it would be fair to say that it isn't getting any easier year by year and he has done it in the modern era. That ensures that he can stand comparison with the best of them.

'He possesses a passion for the game and I always like somebody with passion for the game. His teams always play enterprising football, always want to score goals. He has got a ready smile ... if you don't approach him at the final whistle! He has a good personality.'

Many of the biggest names at the time were linked with the job of England coach when Terry Venables' position become untenable and an announcement over his departure came long before the start of Euro '96. Kevin Keegan and Gerry Francis were among the front runners, but behind the scenes there was an early call to Old Trafford while king-maker Jimmy Armfield was sounding out suitable candidates, including Glenn Hoddle.

Kelly says: 'We approached Manchester United when we were seeking a successor to Terry Venables. I went to Manchester to speak to Martin Edwards. I left it with him and a couple of weeks later he contacted me to inform me that he and his board would not countenance us speaking to Alex. It would have been interesting to have met Alex Ferguson and to have put him alongside Glenn Hoddle ... an interesting situation. I know he would have relished coming down to Lancaster Gate for an interview, but it wasn't to be because he was padlocked at Manchester United. We spoke to Glenn alone.'

The prospect of a Scot in charge of England!

It would have been a thorny issue. Even Hoddle's choice of right-hand man, John Gorman, caused controversy, one of the reasons being that he is a Scot! In a sense it would have been more revolutionary than appointing a foreign coach such as Arsene Wenger or Ruud Gullit.

'Not an issue,' argued Kelly. He explained, 'We were involved in the process of choosing the best man for the job.'

Graham Kelly has a wicked, dry sense of humour and has spoken to Alex many times since. Kelly says: 'Do we mention it? Probably every time I see him!

'Alex got himself a new contract out of it – he owes me a drink for that.

'He wrote about it in his book – he owes me a drink for that.

'I would say we have quite a tie. The sad thing is that I don't drink. I'm sure I can find some way he can show his appreciation for all I've done for him! In fact, I have even picked up the tab for one of his managers' lunches. There was Alex, Howard Wilkinson and a few others at a meeting at the Auderley Edge Hotel where Jimmy Armfield and myself planned to attend in the afternoon. We couldn't make it for lunch so we had to make do with tea and biscuits instead.

'But I decided to pick up the bill for the managers, and only realised how much of a bad move it was to make the grandiose gesture when I saw the bill – they don't stint themselves these guys. That's another one he owes me – with no prospect of collecting on any of them.'

Ferguson has been the central character in the old club-versus-country problem, with a new edge to it with so many of the youngsters nurtured at Old Trafford formulating the essence of the England team under Hoddle.

Ferguson's conflicts with Hoddle are well documented, but Kelly says, 'We have been privileged to be able to choose from so many good young England players and we have clearly benefited from Manchester United's youth policy. Alex Ferguson does not like releasing so many of his players for friendly matches, and quite obviously that creates unease whilst that policy continues. But these are matters for the England coach.'

It would certainly have been interesting to see whether Ferguson's policy would have changed somewhat should he have become the new England coach!

Brian Kidd

Manager, Blackburn Rovers. Former assistant manager, Manchester United. Former England and Manchester United player.

Brian Kidd has spoken for the first time about the Fergie years which forged the most successful partnership in soccer management.

'Kiddo' and 'gaffer' Alex Ferguson won *nine* major trophies in their six sensational years together at Manchester United. That's an incredible silver haul of four Premiership trophies, two FA Cups, the European Cup Winners' Cup, League Cup and European Super Cup.

And now for the first time the former Old Trafford No. 2 reveals the secret of their success.

They both believe in honest principles, drummed into them from the same working-class backgrounds. They had a good laugh together. And they both love a good barney, too, although Kidd is the first to admit that Fergie has mellowed from the blowtorch days of old. He reveals: 'It was good, working with the boss. He has a laugh and, to be fair, he will say his piece. But he doesn't bear any malice. Did we fall out? Loads of times. But let's just say we had discussions.

'When I was youth development officer it was the same. I would have views about certain young players and I would stick to my guns. I wouldn't be overawed or worried about the boss saying what he thought about the player. I would turn back and say, "What do you know? You don't see him enough." He used to laugh at that.

'But fair dos to the boss. If it came to the crunch he would back me.

'Our discussions became very few and far between. In my time with the boss he's certainly mellowed over the last couple of years. Whether that's because we have had a little bit of success, who knows? But whatever the chemistry is, I have certainly enjoyed working with him. You will have to ask him if he enjoyed working with me.'

There was certainly a great bond between them, a partnership that developed into the most formidable of the modern era. But it didn't come easily. They both worked their socks off finding the formula for unprecedented success.

The training ground was their second home – perhaps their first on the days when there was serious work to be done. But rolling their sleeves up is second nature to two men brought up on honest-to-goodness values.

Kidd adds: 'Our backgrounds are similar. I was born in Manchester. Alex was raised in Glasgow. We are both stubborn in certain ways, but we have the same philosophy. You do an honest day's work for an honest day's pay. The boss was brought up by his parents to believe that and so was I. You don't try to short-change anybody.

'We both enjoy our jobs and we don't take them for granted. I loved the working relationship we had.'

Bryan King

Former Millwall goalkeeper. Now scout in Norway.

Alex Ferguson can be expansive, blunt, charming and frightening – all within the same day.

Bryan King lives in Norway where he operates as a part-time talent scout and organiser of tour games for a variety of clubs, and has had many personal dealings with Ferguson which provide an insight into his character. But one of the most amusing he spotted on Norwegian TV when the Manchester United manager was on one of his multitude of overseas spying missions. On this occasion Fergie travelled to Copenhagen just before the World Cup Finals to watch Denmark v. Norway. Ferguson was captured on a TV show knocking on the hotel door of Norway manager Egil Olsen after the game. Fergie looked a little surprised to see Egil's wife and daughter there when he entered the room. The Norwegian manager noticed Ferguson's bewilderment at seeing his family with him at such an important game.

Egil: 'Don't you take your wife to matches?'

Ferguson: 'Never . . . apart from the odd Cup Final.'

Ferguson didn't look too pleased to be on Norwegian TV, particularly as a little later he was spotted by the all-seeing TV camera hobnobbing with notorious soccer agent Rune Hauge and chatting over a cup of coffee with Ronny Johnsen as they discussed his injury problem.

Ferguson has never quite trusted the media, apart from a hand-selected small group of trusted allies.

King said: 'I remember during Alex's early days at Manchester United when he came over to Norway on a scouting mission with his former chief scout Tony Collins, whom he inherited from Ron Atkinson. His mission was to run the rule over a young Norwegian player, Claus

Eftevaag, and we all went to the under-18 international match between Norway and Sweden.

'Alex was very keen to see the player as he knew that Liverpool were also interested. He is extremely methodical and likes his scouting missions.

'We drove to Fredrikstad and saw the game, but found ourselves plagued by journalists who had discovered that Alex was in town – and it was big news. After the game we were meant to have a chat with the boy, but we were engulfed by reporters wherever Alex went both inside and outside the ground.

'In no uncertain terms Alex informed one of the journalists and a photographer precisely where they could stick their pens and cameras . . . a place it would be difficult to remove them from! He was put under pressure but showed great restraint and diplomacy. He just dealt with a very irritating situation in a typically Scottish way.

'Just to cap his day we were stuck in traffic on the way back to Oslo for three and a half hours. Alex asked me if I knew a short cut. "Yes," I told him, "if we had taken a boat!" He replied, "Maybe we should." '

King recommends many players to Premiership clubs but Ferguson prefers to make a judgement based on personal viewing as well as watching videos and reports from his scouts. King said: 'He first watched Henning Berg when he was 17 and wanted to sign him when he saw the potential then but couldn't get a work permit for him.

'Whether he watches a youth team player or an established inter-national, he has the same eye for it, looking for something out of it. He simply has such a great knowledge of the game.

'On a personal level I've probably been very lucky in my dealings with him – I've never got on the wrong side of him. Actually, I think he is a splendid chap. I've always found him to be the sort of bloke who will remember you.'

David Pleat

Tottenham Hotspur director of football. Committee member of the League Managers' Association.

David Pleat is a manager in the Alex Ferguson mould, a grafter who has given his body and soul to the sport, working all hours. Pleat says: 'Alex is a thorough professional, who has been steeped from his early days in the principle of the harder you work the luckier you get!'

In addition to his workload with his club, Ferguson has been an active member of the Managers' Association, his input recognised by fellow committee member Pleat.

'Alex has always taken an active interest in our League Managers' Association affairs since he came down from Scotland, and he has been considered a valued member of the committee. One of his biggest contributions is to defend the rights of lower division managers who have not been treated fairly and who are fighting for adequate compensation. He is the first to support moves by our committee to aid these managers with their legal costs. Alex is always a strong proposer of such items.'

Pleat is often deep in conversation with people inside the game and Ferguson is no exception. Cajoling rather than confrontational, Pleat has helped in some small way to mellow Ferguson. He explains: 'At one stage he was reluctant to loan out players and, to be honest, it was born out of self-protection. But as the years progressed he mellowed a little and accepted the importance to players to gain loan experience. As a consequence he loaned players like David Beckham to Preston, O'Kane to Bury, Thornley to Huddersfield, Appleby to Barnsley, Casper to Bournemouth and Pilkington to Rotherham.

'Give Alex credit, he is prepared to listen to others. I remember that after I left Luton he called me to ask about the merits of Mal Donaghy.

After our chat he signed him for Manchester United and the player continued to provide splendid consistency for three more years at Old Trafford. Never actually a regular in the side, he was nonetheless an important signing at the time, and Alex was even able to sell him on to Chelsea. Alex also called me to discuss the relative qualities of Denis Irwin and Roland Neilson, the outstanding right backs in Division Two when Luton were playing in that division.'

Pleat savours his relationship with Ferguson. Even so, they once had a run-in. Pleat says, 'It was over the price of a player I was trying to buy from him. At a club like Luton we never had enormous resources – certainly compared to Manchester United – and I took issue with him when we were haggling over a mere £20,000. I thought the price he was asking was mean-spirited.'

Pleat always relished his passionate pre-match discussions with his rival manager. He explains: 'Some managers are a bit reluctant to talk to opposing managers before a game, but whenever I went to Old Trafford I always felt comfortable with Alex away from the heat of the dressing room. Between 2.20 p.m. and 2.45 p.m. we would talk about football in general before he would stride into his dressing room to give his last-minute address to his players.'

Pleat's assessment of Ferguson's career is simply glowing. He says: 'Excellent. Why I admire him so much is that he did not have a charismatic playing career. He was, so we are told, a rough, tough striker. But his intelligence in all aspects of the game ensured that he would prove to be a great manager and motivator of men.

'I first had contact with him at Aberdeen and remember well his company in Marseille in 1982 during the European Championship when a party of managers sponsored by Adidas, who supplied their clubs, went to see the game. I have vivid memories of George Courtney going wild with the whistle and creating mayhem in the Spain v. Denmark game. On that trip Alex was a beguiling conversationalist amongst those managers, who included Jim Smith, Jim McLean and Bobby Ferguson. It was then that I knew that Alex was ambitious, held strong opinions and could relate to life . . .'

Irving Scholar

Ex-Tottenham chairman. Now part-owner and director of football of Nottingham Forest.

Irving Scholar often fantasises how he might have changed the course of soccer history by recruiting Alex Ferguson as manager at Tottenham Hotspur. For the first time Scholar provides the true inside tale of how he courted and won Ferguson, only to lose him on a technicality. In fact, Ferguson had given his word and had shaken hands with Scholar on a 'done deal' to become the new boss of White Hart Lane after Keith Burkinshaw.

In Maddox Street off Oxford Street, Scholar retains his central London offices as a base, although he resides in Monte Carlo. He took great pride in Dave Bassett's exploits at Forest where, since he became part of the take-over, the ailing club launched a successful promotion campaign, finishing as champions. It was a personally satisfying return to soccer after selling Spurs to Alan Sugar and Terry Venables. When Bassett had to leave there was great sadness at the club.

Still a Spurs fan through and through, Scholar orchestrated an amazing coup at Spurs to take control in time for the UEFA Cup triumph in the early '80s, but it was clear that manager Keith Burkinshaw had reached the end of his reign at the club, irrespective of landing the European trophy at the end of his farewell season.

Scholar, the power and influence behind the then chairman Douglas Alexiou, went in search of the man he believed would secure Spurs' future as one of the Big Five clubs at the time – Alex Ferguson.

Scholar recalls: 'Keith Burkinshaw wanted to leave at the end of the season; he had made that clear. A very important decision had to be made, as it always it when a manager leaves. There was one person at the time who looked to be one of the real up-and-coming stars of the game – Alex Ferguson at Aberdeen. His record in Scotland was nothing short of exceptional. He was the first manager in modern times to break the Old Firm stranglehold, and in addition to that achieved something that very few Scottish managers had ever done, which was to win a European trophy when Aberdeen beat Real Madrid in the final of the Cup Winners' Cup. Even so, he was not really recognised at the time by people south of the border, and would not have been someone who would have readily sprung to mind as a manager for a club in England. Yet it seemed to be an opportunity that one had to try to explore.

'Quietly I sounded him out to see whether he would even give consideration to the possibility of coming to Spurs. I had heard one or two whispers on the grapevine that maybe it would be a possibility. Strangely enough, we played Bayern Munich that season in the UEFA Cup and the president of the German club spoke with clear admiration of Alex Ferguson as a potential future Bayern manager! His reputation had begun to spread into Europe.

'I was delighted to discover when I did sound him out through some associates of mine that Alex Ferguson's response was positive.' Scholar and Ferguson selected a suitable venue. Ferguson travelled to Paris from Aberdeen, while Scholar travelled from Monaco.

Scholar details the first time they got together to discuss the move to Spurs. Scholar says: 'A meeting was arranged out of the way in Paris so we wouldn't be recognised or hassled. I spent a day listening to his thoughts and aspirations relating purely to football. He was an interesting character and clearly very hungry to succeed in the future. The meeting went exceptionally well and I felt an immediate affinity with him. He gave me the distinct impression that he was a very clear thinker who knew what he wanted and how he would go about getting it; he had the ability to fill you with confidence. You just knew that wherever he went, he would succeed in the future.

'Over the ensuing few weeks the discussions quietly continued, finally reaching a point where all outstanding matters, financial and otherwise, had been settled and there were no matters left open apart from the signature on the contract.

'Alex made it clear from the very beginning that he wanted the late Dick Donald, the Aberdeen chairman at the time, whom he saw very much as a father figure, to be taken into consideration. He felt that the whole affair had to be handled very delicately with the club because of his special relationship with the chairman. He didn't want to let him or the club down. I respected that. In fact, I admired it. Nevertheless, matters progressed and there was a further meeting with him in Paris. This time I brought along another Spurs director at that time.

'It was at this meeting that Alex Ferguson and I finally shook hands on the agreement that he would become our next Spurs manager. Discussions would then commence with Aberdeen and it would be announced early in the summer of '84. During all our discussions we both made it clear that once we'd shaken hands there would be no going back. I was to be alerted by Alex exactly when would be the most appropriate time to make the formal approach to Aberdeen, but it was also agreed that he would lay the ground in advance.'

However, everything didn't go according to plan or to the agreement thrashed out with a final handshake in Paris. Scholar was shocked when suddenly it all went pear-shaped. As the season was about to close, Spurs knew that behind the scenes they had lined up their replacement for Burkinshaw. Or so they thought. Scholar continued: 'Unfortunately, Alex Ferguson finally advised me in May that he couldn't go ahead with it because he felt he would be letting his chairman down.'

Well, he certainly let Spurs and Scholar down.

But to Scholar's eternal credit, he refused to make any fuss. None of the details have come to light, and he has never had a bad word for Ferguson even though he has every right to have felt aggrieved.

Scholar is a close friend of the Manchester United chairman, Martin Edwards. Scholar was delighted when Ferguson brought so much success to Old Trafford, but he couldn't resist telling his pal Martin about his attempts to sign Ferguson himself. Scholar recalls Edwards's amazement. 'Alex hadn't been the manager at Old Trafford very long when I told Martin Edwards that Alex had actually shaken hands with me on an agreement to become Spurs' manager. Initially he couldn't believe it and rang me a couple of weeks later; he had asked Alex whether it was true. Bearing in mind Alex is such a stickler about his word being his bond and not letting people down, Martin was convinced that Alex wouldn't agree with my version of events. Martin told me that Alex's reaction when he confronted him with it said it all!'

Scholar applauds Martin for sticking with Ferguson after four barren years and when the fans were calling for the manager's head. Scholar says: 'Martin, like myself, had enormous faith in Alex and even when things were not going well he stood firmly behind him, ignoring at times quite vociferous supporters who wanted him sacked.

'In fact, I remember clearly one game that Spurs played at Old Trafford in a League Cup tie in September 1989. It was the day Terry Fenwick broke his leg. We beat United 3–0, with Gary Lineker getting one of the goals, and the atmosphere among the crowd was so hostile at the end of the match that when Martin Edwards was walking down the directors' box to the exit two or three fans tried to climb a barrier to attack him. I was walking right behind him. He was lucky they were intercepted in time by security men. Strangely enough, that was the last time they lost a cup tie at Old Trafford that season as they went on to lift the FA Cup in May.'

He has naturally followed the progress of Ferguson with great interest. He says: 'Alex is in a way a manager ahead of his time. He is a great admirer of the European style of football. When we met in Paris first of all to discuss his ideas on the game, he was talking clearly of the mixture of Continental skills and how they can be combined with the best part of the English game, and how if they could be integrated you would have a highly successful team in a very modern style. That is what Alex set out to accomplish and he achieved just that.

'I remember ringing Martin Edwards after Manchester United finally broke their 26-year duck and won the championship, and I said to him, "Now you've managed to achieve it once, I'm absolutely certain you will go on and repeat it two or three times." A lot of credit should go to the board of Manchester United for that, and to Martin in particular because it's normal in this game for supporters to get the manager sacked, but they stood firm and had belief in Alex's ability and their own judgement and they have been proved one hundred per cent correct.'

Scholar has met Ferguson on occasion since they met in Paris. 'Yes, I have bumped into him quite a few times, and I would say that we have remained friends. In fact, I rang him for advice when we were going to buy Richard Gough. I said to him, "You know the Scottish scene better than anybody ..." I felt I could trust his judgement and trust that he would give me a valid assessment. He told me all about Richard Gough. He told me, "Richard is a big winner in Scotland and if you could get him, don't hesitate." I never hesitated and a few days later Richard Gough signed for Spurs.'

Alan Sugar

Spurs chairman. Amstrad chairman.

Friend of Margaret Thatcher, captain of industry, the 55th richest man in the UK, upwardly mobile in the recently published *Sunday Times* list of the biggest bank accounts in the country, Alan Sugar is one of the most influential and powerful men of his generation.

After eight years in soccer Sugar has learned more than he imagined there was to discover about a simple sport. Now Sugar is wiser and more profound on the subject, so when he endorses Alex Ferguson's credentials as a managerial icon he knows what he's talking about.

Sugar says: 'Alex Ferguson has my utmost admiration for what he has achieved at Manchester United. Frankly I can't say I know him well. I've met him on two or three occasions and spoken to him for no more than a combined hour. Even so, it was long enough for Alex to make a firm impression on me. He had a very, very shrewd look about him; he looked as though he was in total control, and of course he is. He deserves your respect for his achievements alone.

'But he struck me as a personality and a character most unlike the popular view of him. I enjoyed our little chats and found him a man with a good sense of humour who enjoyed a laugh and a joke.

'It may be that so many people find him abrasive because they continually harass him with questions about the obvious. You know how it goes, "Are you going to win the title?" "Will Manchester United win the cup?" It's the sort of thing, if you're asked often enough, that's bound to be infuriating. Perhaps we enjoyed a reasonable rapport because I asked him about things unconnected to winning the championship or the FA Cup.

'Jokingly, I asked him how he has managed to pinch so many talented youngsters from under our noses – don't forget that David Beckham was first associated with our club. He retorted by wanting to know how we got one or two that he'd wanted! It was all good banter and he was able to laugh about it. There were certainly no hostilities whenever we met.'

As for Ferguson's attributes as a successful manager, Sugar has been naturally impressed by his work rate, commitment to the club's cause and, of course, a net return in terms of tangible assets – silverware. Sugar says: 'He is a very hard-working person and has built a successful team without breaking the Bank of England to do it. Far too often fans think the only solution is to throw money at it, but Alex Ferguson has proved that a club needs a foundation based on a youth structure and we are trying to do that at Spurs with our own academy of football.

'He commands respect from his players. You never hear of a Manchester United player mouthing off in the media about their manager and his methods, and he also comes across as a shrewd and knowledgeable football man whenever he is interviewed on television.

'But most important is his record. We can all talk day and night about our ideas and ways of doing things. It's incredible what Alex Ferguson has achieved. The bottom line is the record speaks for itself.'

Gordon Taylor

Chief executive, Professional Footballers' Association.

Manchester-based players' union leader Gordon Taylor is highly complimentary of Alex Ferguson as a man and a manager.

That might come as a surprise to some for the pair have had their run-ins in the past, on one occasion bordering on the violent, but Taylor bears no grudges and he hopes that Ferguson feels the same. If anything, Taylor's admiration for Ferguson has increased.

He talks in nothing but glowing terms about Fergie. 'I have to say I am a big admirer of Alex Ferguson and the job he's done both at Manchester United and Aberdeen. He is the most successful manager ever to come to England from Scotland.

'I have been particularly impressed by his youth policy at Old Trafford. It is the perfect model for every other big club in the game. Even though the club has such mammoth resources they have periodically developed their own home-produced players when they could have bought in players from any part of the world. It has certainly paid off with the Neville brothers, Beckham, Butt, Scholes and Giggs, with other top-quality youngsters coming through now.'

On a personal level, Taylor says: 'Alex is a very strong-minded individual. He is not only captain of his ship but he also wants to know everything that is going on in his ship – that's the way he has always run things.

'Alex always remembers his grass roots from Glasgow, his trade union background. He has been a big supporter of the Scottish PFA and he supports us whenever we ask him. He was our guest of honour at one of our awards dinners.

'Of course, being the personalities that we are, we are both very passionate about the game. We have had our clashes and agreed to disagree at times. Yes, we have been close to coming to blows, but we haven't quite!'

Ferguson and Taylor clashed during England's match against Switzerland at Wembley in November 1995. In fact, there is no other way to describe it, other than two of the most prominent figures in football locked in an eyeball-to-eyeball slanging match. The row was over the Manchester United manager's video which featured Ferguson criticising Alan Shearer for being greedy in his wage demands. Ferguson criticised Shearer in the video for putting money first by joining Blackburn rather than Manchester United.

Taylor's job is to defend his players, and will do so as fiercely as possible when he believes it warrants it. Taylor publicly called for Fergie to face a disrepute charge after reading about the video in the press. When the two met at Wembley shortly afterwards tempers boiled over. Taylor waited until the area by Wembley's banqueting hall was quiet before approaching Ferguson. But the argument, which took place at the start of the second half, was witnessed by at least one FA official. The two men had hoped their clash would remain private, but the fact that it leaked out was embarrassing for both of them.

Fergie had launched the video in Manchester and travelled to London for promotional work. Taylor, asked to comment on the video, said that Paul McGrath had been found guilty of bringing the game into disrepute after remarks about Ferguson in his book, and so Ferguson should be brought to task for making adverse comments about Shearer. Taylor spotted Ferguson at Wembley and decided to explain his views. Ferguson's language was typically forceful and the situation developed into an amazing scene. Ferguson never commented on the outburst.

Taylor looks back, not in anger but on an episode long forgotten – hopefully forgiven. He says: 'Grudges? I hope not. We have clashed at times. We had our disagreements over work permits for certain players and over disciplinary matters. He is a very strong supporter of his players, and at times there have been some very delicate issues to sort out. One naturally springs to mind – the problems with the Wright and Schmeichel affair.

'We had our differences when Alex was the subject of criticism when Paul McGrath left the club. There was a problem with Norman Whiteside and Paul McGrath having a worrying clique at the club and Bryan Robson. Alex felt that both Norman and McGrath ought to consider retirement because of their injuries. That was like a cold bath to McGrath as he wanted to carry on. But there were deep concerns about his fitness and whether he was looking after himself properly.' That is soccer-speak for a drinking problem. Taylor, however, was being diplomatic.

He went on: 'A decision was taken by Paul that he didn't want to retire and take a settlement but wanted the opportunity to join another club and, of course, he went on to continue his career with Aston Villa and the Republic of Ireland. It worked out well for Paul in the end but he was upset about leaving Manchester. He made some critical remarks and Alex was naturally concerned about them and very sensitive about them. A complaint was lodged with the Football Association. Paul was found guilty and fined a considerable amount of money.'

But the issue of the Ferguson video made the sparks fly at Wembley. 'Alex made references on the video to players who had left the club, like Paul Ince and Andrei Kanchelskis, and also commented about why Shearer didn't go to the club. I felt there were sensitive circumstances about why players had left the club and that he ought to be careful about remarks concerning players no longer at the club.

'How did my remarks about Alex go down? They went down like a sack of King Edwards! The result was the altercation at Wembley, where I had to stand my ground. It didn't come to blows. Nearly. But not quite.'

Whatever has occurred in the past, Taylor's admiration for Ferguson is undiminished. 'Our relationship is fine. I would like to think there is mutual respect for each other. I've been particularly impressed by the way he looks after players who have fallen on hard times. David Busst is a case in point. He is always willing to bring down his team for a testimonial for a worthy cause, despite a congested fixture list – one aspect of the man that isn't lauded around. That is a sign of the bloke's charity.'

AGENTS

Jerome Anderson

Jerome Anderson Associates. FIFA licensed soccer agent.

Jerome Anderson operates his agency, together with Geoff Weston, in Edgware so there's no guessing that he's an Arsenal fan.

Anderson recalls: 'I was introduced to Alex through my very close friendship with Charlie Nicholas when Alex was still manager at Aberdeen. Charlie mentioned to me that he thought I should meet the man who would one day become a very successful manager south of the border. He was right.

'The first time I met him I came away with a feeling that this guy was very passionate about the game. It was a very warm meeting, and we talked about many aspects of football.

'Alex has become a great manager in England because he brought his expertise from Aberdeen and he has such vast knowledge of the game. His commitment to Manchester United is unflinching.'

Anderson then developed a professional relationship with Ferguson. 'He worked tirelessly to get United back on track, and you have to admire the way he built up the club from youth level upwards. The result is that the club possess one of the best group of home-grown youngsters this country has ever seen. In his early days we dealt with Lee Sharpe and Russell Beardsmore on Alex's go-ahead. He knows we do a good job with these players, although we did cross swords on just one problem that occurred with Lee Sharpe.

'Lee wanted to play abroad and he asked us to examine the possibilities for him. There were people at that time interested, but they asked him to put his name to an agreement, a sort of confirmation that he would be interested. When Alex found out he wasn't amused, to say the least – that would be the best way of putting it.

'With Alex you know exactly where you stand. What you see is what you get. I admire the unbelievable successes he has achieved at Old Trafford so you cannot knock his methods. He's a winner, an out-and-out winner.'

Dennis Roach

PRO International. FIFA licensed soccer agent.

Dennis Roach is one of the top soccer agents in the world, whose clients include the former England coach Glenn Hoddle and one of Manchester United's former heroes, Mark Hughes.

He says: 'It has to be said that Alex and I have never been the best of buddies, although I don't know why. When we meet socially we get on fine but businesswise it has always proved somewhat difficult. I think the problem dates back to when Alex first took over as manager of Manchester United from Ron Atkinson. At the time I had a very close relationship not only with Ron but also chairman Martin Edwards. Perhaps Alex thought it was probably too close.

'It's a matter of record what Alex has achieved and I think, like any manager taking on the Manchester United job, he struggled at first but managed to get through those early stages, and now his achievements can only be described as magnificent. He was fortunate in inheriting the exciting youth team from Brian Whitehouse, but he has had the intelligence to groom, manage and steer those youngsters from the youth team into the first team, and that shows the area of his real quality. He has a record of looking after and caring for people, not just the youngsters but also his staff, and I think that shows in the way that on every occasion he gave his assistant Brian Kidd excellent praise for his part in the work that has been done – and, let's face it, Brian Kidd deserves it.'

Roach brought Mark Hughes back to Old Trafford from Barcelona, and then eventually played his role in the sale to Chelsea. He recalls: 'Mark had an offer of a five-year contract to sign for Bayern Munich after going there on loan, but it was at the time he was marrying his fiancée Gill. As he told me, it was his one opportunity of going back to Manchester United and he wanted to take it.

'For some unknown reason Mark seemed to rub Alex up the wrong way, although this is something that Alex always denies. Yet Mark always said that if Manchester United were to lose 3–2 away from home and he'd scored the two goals, Alex would have blamed him for the three goals conceded!

'I've come round to Mark's way of thinking when you look at the way that, over a period, he has been left out of important games, and there have been occasions when his absence has surprised the pundits and experts. One of those times was in the Champions' League game in Turkey when United lost to Galatasaray and Mark was left out when most people thought that game was made for Mark.

'Overall, Mark got on well with Alex, but there came a time when he felt he was not getting a regular place in the side, very similar to the reasons behind his recent move from Chelsea to Southampton. There came a point at Old Trafford where he felt it was time to move on. Glenn Hoddle made an approach and he decided to move to Stamford Bridge.

'Manchester United had been very good to Mark with a testimonial, but he wanted regular football. To be fair to Alex and Martin Edwards, the club were terrific in assisting with that chance to move by asking only a moderate fee of £1.5 million.'

Jon Smith

First Artist Management. FIFA licensed soccer agent.

The Smith brothers, Jon and Phil, have a long list of high-profile soccer stars on their books, and as a consequence deal with virtually all the managers in the game. Alex Ferguson hadn't been at Old Trafford long before one of the Smiths' 'clients' was being snapped up from Middlesbrough – Gary Pallister. It was to become a benchmark signing in football – a record fee for a defender – but, as Jon discloses, it was even more significant than that for Ferguson.

Jon recalls: 'The final meeting to clinch the deal took place, of all places, in a windswept car park at the back of a pub at Scotts Corner just outside Middlesbrough ... It was a revolting day but for some reason this was the only venue that we all came up with to maintain a degree of confidentiality. Bruce Rioch got out of his car and Alex, Gary and myself got out of our car. Bruce Rioch came up to the three of us and the first thing he said as he pointed to me was, "You can fuck off." That's all he ever said to me in the entire transaction. I think Bruce had an aversion to soccer agents! He wouldn't deal with me throughout the weeks of talks and the only contact I had with his club was through his board of directors.

'But to Alex's credit, he responded on my behalf. He told Bruce, "No, he's part of the deal." It took three hours to thrash out the deal. Gary desperately wanted to sign for Manchester United, but Boro were holding out for a massive fee at that time.

'When it was all finished, Alex put his arm around my shoulder and confessed that he felt that a record £2.3 million for a defender was a huge gamble. At that time the money *was* huge, and the reaction massive.

'He said he had put himself on the line. "I don't believe I've paid so much for him," he told me. He was really reluctant to pay that much but it was the only way to get the player he really wanted.

'Alex went on, "If I get this one wrong I'm for the chop." At the time his team was not doing all that well, and he knew that signing Gary Pallister was a big, big risk for him.

'It's ironic that now Alex has spent another record fee on another centre half when he bought Jaap Stam from PSV Eindhoven for £10.75 million.'

Jon's next major connection with Ferguson came when he was assigned the job of running the Manchester United's 'players' pool' for the FA Cup Final with Crystal Palace – a critical time for the Manchester United manager as this was to be his breakthrough trophy.

Jon recalls: 'This was the turning point for Alex, and I was with him all the time in the build-up to the final. There was no question that his job was on the line again.

'Danny McGregor, the commercial director, turned to me when United won the replay and said, "That's it, now we're going to be successful." From that moment Alex and his team never looked back and nor has the club.'

Jon has experienced the Ferguson mood swings. He says: 'Yes, Alex can be very unpredictable. One moment he is sweetness and light, the next moment he can explode over the smallest thing.

'The Manchester United team were billeted in the same hotel that the England team now use, the Burnham Beeches, in preparation for the FA Cup Final with Palace. The sponsors wanted one final picture on the day before the big game. The team bus arrived back at the hotel after training and the photographer was waiting outside the hotel for his picture. The players accommodatingly got off the bus and were ready for the picture shoot. But not Alex. He was supposed to be in the picture but he wouldn't get off the bus until he had finished his game of cards! When someone went on the coach to ask him to come off he snapped, "No, I'm not ready."

'Alex stayed on the bus playing cards with some of the players and wouldn't let them go until he had won his hand – no matter how long it took or how long everyone was left waiting for him. We all had to wait for 20 minutes. Finally Alex disembarked from the coach, having won his hand. Now he was all sweetness and light.'

Jon has nothing but admiration for the way Ferguson rules the

Old Trafford dressing room with a rod of iron. He says, 'He is very authoritative. There is a commanding air about him.

'I really have enjoyed working with him over the years, and I have learned an awful lot from him, particularly how to deal with people.'

THE MEDIA

Trevor Brooking

BBC Match of the Day. *Ex-West Ham and England.*

Trevor Brooking is such a laid-back character one could hardly imagine him crossing swords with even the volatile Alex Ferguson. And, of course, he hasn't. But he has met him away from the tension of a game scenario and was impressed by his off-the-field demeanour. Brooking says: 'The only time I've seen him in a relaxed mode was when he came out for the Italy–England game in Rome and we were in the same hotel reception before the big match. It was the first time I had seen him in an environment when he was not thinking about participating in a game and he looked extremely relaxed.

'I've heard he has a good sense of humour and the people he trusts see a different side to his character and personality than the one generally given to the public. He is also a very loyal person. You can see that when he is intensely protective of his players and the club in general.'

Brooking has no doubts about Ferguson's pedigree as a manager. Analysing the Manchester United manager's achievements, he said: 'Yes, I would say he must be regarded as a "great" manager. I don't think there can be any real question about that. He transformed both Aberdeen and then Manchester United.

'I think that Manchester United were a massive club that were under-achievers and are now a financial empire with fantastic foundations for continuing their success. The strength of their youth structure makes them a magnet for all the best young talent throughout the country.'

Brooking knows that Ferguson won't rest until he wins the Champions' League. He says: 'Alex has won titles, cups and plenty of personal accolades and honours, but the icing on the cake would be the Champions' League and I don't think he will be satisfied until he wins it. There have been rumours once or twice that he will pack it up. From a personal point of view I believe he will be reluctant to relinquish the reins until he has won the Champions' League.'

He doesn't under-estimate the importance of discipline that is reflected in the way that Ferguson and his players look whenever they travel abroad, representing themselves, their club and their country. 'All the players dress and behave in a correct manner, and I feel that says a lot about the discipline within the club and that the manager places an importance about how his players appear. The way the players look reflects the authority that Ferguson exercises within the club. I would go as far as to say that the Manchester United players and club are the most impressive travelling group from this country.'

Brooking is renowned for being non-controversial, but whether it's on *Football Focus*, *Match of the Day* or Radio Five Live, the former Hammers idol has more to say than most people would imagine. He's not afraid to discuss the downside to the Ferguson persona. He doesn't disagree, for example, that a great deal of the lack of popularity for Manchester United, despite an exciting and entertaining playing philosophy, stems from the manager whinging about decisions that go against the team, in addition to his refusal to give the opposition much credit. In short he is a bad loser.

Brooking argues: 'It is a shame if it is the case that the club's unpopularity among rival fans stems from the manager. Perhaps Alex does need to loosen up now and again! Unfortunately Alex is a public figure who has a poor public image to a certain extent. There is an element of Alex begrudging opponents success; he can come across as a dour individual.

'I find it all very strange for someone who supposedly is so experienced with the media. He could handle the media a little bit more affably than he does. All right, we live in a world that rewards winners. Alex is a winner. He has got all the plaudits he deserves for his achievements, and he has been a winner because of that outward intensity.'

Sometimes the intensity goes overboard. United are envied, in much the same way as Liverpool were at the height of their success, but Ferguson's offhand approach has played a role in increasing dislike of a club that has a brand of football of which the country ought to be proud. Brooking went on: 'Yes, at times Alex's attitude works against them. It's such a shame because they are a good footballing side, good to watch and highly entertaining. The fans' dislike cannot be anything to do with what happens on the playing side. Of course, there is always a lot of envy around when any club is successful. They are the ones they love to criticise, and it did also happen with Liverpool.'

Garth Crooks

BBC Match of the Day *interviewer. Former Spurs, Manchester United and Stoke striker.*

Garth Crooks is one of a handful of former professionals who have moved across to the media and become highly successful, giving them a completely new perspective of the way those inside the game handle the media.

Ferguson is one of the more difficult of those in the game to deal with. Crooks explains: 'Everybody is on tenterhooks when the press corps arrive at Manchester United, either at the training ground or at Old Trafford, if you know you have to deal with Alex Ferguson. You know in advance that if you ask a sharp question you will get a sharp answer. Personally I wouldn't expect anything else from him if I asked a sharp question.

'But I like him, I must say. I like him very much. I feel he is very fair and consistent ... at least, he has been with me! I've had no problems with him whatsoever. In fact, I have found him to be perfectly charming – I hope it stays that way.'

There are two anecdotes that Garth enjoys relating – one good, one not so good. He says: 'There was one time when I arrived at Old Trafford to do an interview with him, totally unannounced, and you are always apprehensive about that. Manchester United had been drawn against Borussia Dortmund in the Champions' League semi-finals and it was important to get the United manager to comment. But he didn't want to know. Instead of agreeing to my request for an interview on the *Football Focus* programme, he stuck by his prior arrangement to carry on with a local radio interview. Alex refused to do the interview with me, but he did allow me to interview the players, and I was grateful for that. As I said, tough but fair.

'Yet there was another occasion when I interrupted him with his family and friends having a meal at Old Trafford when there was a Simply Red concert on, and he not only agreed to my request for an interview – again not pre-arranged – he even apologised for keeping me waiting! I never thought I would get the interview but I explained that there was no other time to do it and promised him it would only take a few minutes. The camera crew thought I had no chance as well. But the crew almost fell over when someone came out of the restaurant and said Fergie would be ready in about five minutes. We hung around. It was a nightmare because no one really thought he would come out and do the interview, and would just walk away instead. To be honest, he would have been justified in doing so. But out he came, did the interview and was perfectly charming. Then he went back to his dinner. That is the side of Alex Ferguson that I should imagine few people experience ... Admittedly, Manchester United had just won the championship!'

Crooks's assessment of Ferguson's career is glowing. He says: 'He must be one of the top all-time managers the UK has produced. He's up there with the best, like Paisley, Stein, Shankly and Sir Matt.'

Steve Curry

Sunday Telegraph *soccer writer. Sky TV.*

For 30 years associated with the *Daily Express*, where he was their long-serving chief football correspondent before switching to the Sunday paper, Steve Curry struck up a close relationship with Alex Ferguson.

As a United fan, his heart is very much at Old Trafford, and his admiration and respect for Ferguson unflinching. He is passionate about the club and their manager.

He says: 'Ferguson has proved himself one of the great managers. When you list the men who have made the biggest impact on the domestic game you talk in terms of Bill Shankly, you talk of Jock Stein and of Sir Matt Busby and you talk of Bob Paisley ... You also talk of Ferguson. Since the First Division became the Premiership his club has dominated football, and in truth he has done that in the way he has completely restructured Manchester United. That marks him down as a great manager.

'There had been a succession of managers in the wake of Busby, none of whom could handle making United a great club again. Alex started from scratch by scrapping the youth system and setting up his own as he was determined that Manchester United would attract the best kids around. For the past two to three seasons we have seen the benefits of all that hard work, with the Neville brothers, Scholes, Butt and Beckham coming through. He has spent heavily at times but generally the mark of his great achievement is building a new team based on the young players.

'To put him right at the top of the tree he needs to win the European Cup, and that is the one remaining ambition of his. If he won the European Cup he would step down, in my opinion. But he has still got the energy and drive – in fact, he has amazing energy. He is still the first person to arrive at the training ground each morning, with the exception of the tea lady, and that is a measure of what he puts into that job. He is in the mould of the great Scottish managers, who've possessed that great work ethic as they've come from nothing through to the top.

'He is one of the last of a particular breed of manager, along with Ron Atkinson. He is a hands-on manager – nothing is done at Old Trafford on the playing side without Ferguson's involvement. Ferguson still does it in the old way – even if the kids need a new kit he has to know about it and it goes through him. That is no longer the trend. Now coaches concentrate on preparing and selecting the team and that's all. When it's time for Fergie to leave they will not appoint another like him.

'He has his faults. Sometimes he is blind to the frailties of some people at United, but he is fiercely loyal to his players. He can be an abrasive man; if you cross Ferguson he'll tell you about it in no uncertain terms.

'I feel the kind of football Manchester United play and try to play under Ferguson is an attacking, entertaining style and that's why Ferguson finds it very difficult to understand the anti-Manchester United feeling that exists around the country. The reason is that the club is so successful, not because of him. Also there is this firm belief that it is not really a Manchester club because of supporters from all around the country that gravitate to Old Trafford and to the away games, but that started with the Munich air crash which brought so much public sympathy from all over the country and made people lean towards Manchester United. However badly or well Manchester United are doing, they are always a well-supported club.

'He has had his moments of good fortune. Eric Cantona was the catalyst, the last piece of the jigsaw for the first championship, and he got him by a fluke.

'Howard Wilkinson rang Fergie to ask him if he would sell Denis Irwin. He replied, "I won't sell Denis, but how about selling me Cantona?" He picked up Cantona for £1 million on a whim and it was the signing that was the catalyst for all the young players. Sometimes a make-or-break situation can happen like that, and it did for Ferguson.'

Steve has been in a privileged position, a confidant of Ferguson's, and there are precious few journalists afforded such an honour. There are many anecdotes about Ferguson that he would rather remained confidential, and that is the kind of fierce loyalty that marks out Ferguson's friends. When Steve left the *Express* after such a lengthy stint it was Ferguson who was there for him. Steve recalls: 'He was one of the first on the phone, and that shows he cares. He is a compassionate man.'

Colin Gibson

Sports editor of the Sunday Telegraph.

'Picture the scene. Manchester United have just won their first championship for 26 years. The long wait is over. For most managers it would have been an excuse to bathe in the warmth of the glory. Not Alex Ferguson.

'When Manchester United triumphed in May 1993, Alex Ferguson could have been forgiven for believing that his life's work was complete. United's fans had grown impatient waiting for that success.

'The longer the time went without a championship the more the triumphs of the Sir Matt Busby era weighed heavily on the shoulders of the next generation of players. Now, though, Ferguson had delivered the Holy Grail to Old Trafford. But it was not enough. Winning alone, you see, has never been satisfying for Ferguson. A fleeting glimpse of the summit of English football was not what Ferguson planned. He wanted Manchester United to set up camp on the summit and repel all rivals for the foreseeable future. So what happened in the hours after that championship triumph explain why Ferguson became the greatest manager in modern English football.

'Oh, he did allow himself to drink in the enormity of his achievement. We dined two days later amidst the glitterati of London society but you could tell he was anxious to return to his workshop. That has always been the Cliff training ground where Ferguson decided to groom a succession of young players for the great stage of Old Trafford – the Theatre of Dreams.

'And this was the reason for the dash back to Manchester. The championship may have been won but the future still had to be secured.

'While many other managers rarely take notice of their youth teams, let alone bother watching them, Ferguson has paid meticulous attention to the development of youngsters at Manchester United. On a dark and dank January day, when success was still a distant oasis, Ferguson outlined his philosophy.

' "It is no good building a side that can win just one title. You have to build a dynasty." And that is what Ferguson achieved. He recognised at Aberdeen that by producing home-grown talent you can not only save a fortune in the transfer market but also guarantee the future of a football club.

'What was happening on that May evening in 1993? The Manchester United youth team were playing in the FA Youth Cup final against Leeds. United lost but while that may have hurt for a moment Ferguson knew what talent he had discovered.

' "Look at that young boy, the one with the red hair. He is the closest thing I have ever seen to a young Kenny Dalglish." The boy was Paul Scholes. "He'll play for England one day," confirmed Ferguson. Not only did Scholes play for England but so did some of his other team-mates in that youth side. There was Gary and Philip Neville, Nicky Butt and a certain David Beckham. If anything, English football owes a debt to Alex Ferguson.'

Brian Glanville

Correspondent for The Sunday Times

'Is Alex Ferguson one of the great British managers, or does he, perhaps, just miss? His achievements are beyond doubt. After those long, bleak years in which Manchester United, almost inexplicably, failed to win a championship which had last been theirs in 1967, he established them almost as monopolists of the title. He twice won the European Cup Winners' Cup, on the first occasion – an astonishing feat – with Scotland's Aberdeen, a David-and-Goliath affair, overshadowing even Manchester United's fine victory that night in Barcelona.

'Obliged, like all British club managers, to be a veritable polymath, master of all aspects – at times tactician, psychologist, dealer in the transfer market – he pulled off what was surely one of the major coups of all football time when he picked up Eric Cantona for not much more than a million from Leeds; and contrived to keep him. Howard Wilkinson had simply given up on the preposterously talented, preposterously pretentious, endlessly moody Frenchman, which was why he let him go for so little. Ferguson not only gambled; he made sure the gamble worked. Until the night at Selhurst Park of the notorious kung-fu kick, Cantona was the motor and the inspiration of United's feats in League and Cup.

'And yet ... And yet ... Given the immense financial clout of the club, should United, under Ferguson, not have achieved even more? Was one of their championships not won almost by default when Newcastle United, a so much more attractive side then, suddenly fell apart? Should United not have stayed the course and taken the title last season, when around Christmas the Mancunian bookies were refusing to take any more bets on them? Instead of falling apart themselves, even belying their superb performance at Chelsea in the FA Cup, allowing an Arsenal team which looked not even a remote outsider to canter past them on the last laps?

'And what can one say of a great club when a player, Russia's Kanchelskis, misdiagnosed, has to go to United's former, defenestrated, physio to have his injury properly diagnosed and treated? What of Ferguson's strange, ambivalent, surely self-destructive treatment of Mark Hughes, forever being dropped when he was clearly so important to the side (not least in a lost League match at Chelsea), and finally being sold to Chelsea themselves? With Ferguson pleading feebly that he'd been abroad at the time and knew nothing about it.

'Tactically, he can often be faulted. Such as with the game in Turin when Cantona, no speedster, was stuck alone up front and the advantage handed to a Juventus team, which gladly grabbed it. The European Cup, which Busby at last won, continues to elude Ferguson. Last season, not least after a fine win over Juve at Old Trafford, things ended with a whimper. Defeat in Turin, enabling Juve to squeeze into the next round. Dullness in Monaco on a pitch where Juve did not find it hard to play; dull defeat at home. Just not good enough.

'And he is so thin-skinned, so easily provoked. So harsh, at times, on local journalists, who can't fight back. An image. After a match against Liverpool. Ferguson lamenting a supposed injustice. Kenny Dalglish, no friend to the press himself, went by with his baby daughter in his arms and said, "You'll get more sense out of her!"

'Ferguson is a loyal, honest, passionate man, loyal to his shipyard roots, once a determined rather than a gifted centre forward, still good enough to lead the Rangers attack. Humorous in private, dour and sometimes touchy in his public persona. As in his strange feud with Alan Green, the BBC radio commentator; one surely symptomatic. I think I know what happened, and am not going to involve myself in an exegesis. Sufficient to say that from Ferguson's huge height, radio commentators, however supposedly turbulent, should surely be majestically ignored, if not forgiven.

'A great manager, then, or simply a very good one?'

Andy Gray

Sky TV. Ex-Scotland, Aston Villa and Everton.

Andy Gray once dared to suggest live on Sky Sport that Manchester United won penalty favours from referees. He didn't quite put it like that, but that's how Alex Ferguson interpreted it. The result was a TV row that would ensure Sky's ratings!

Andy has broken new ground with Sky television, love or loathe his methods. He has made an impact with his knack for new technology which has inspired a TV commercial.

He is also not afraid to speak his mind. When he felt that Barnsley deserved a penalty against United, he said so, but then he suggested that had it been an appeal for a penalty by Manchester United they would have got it.

As a player, I remember Andy as a fearless, fearsome centre forward in the old-fashioned mould, and as a TV analyst he has that same abrasive edge that makes him compulsive viewing. You have to be brave to take on Fergie!

Andy recalls: 'What can I say about Fergie? Well, the Barnsley game last year just about sums him up. I was analysing the game afterwards when I said what about 99 per cent of the viewers were no doubt thinking anyway – I wondered if it had happened at the other end whether Manchester United would have been given a penalty.

'What I didn't know was that as soon as the game was over Alex went straight from the touchline to his room, switched on the telly and heard my analysis of the penalty. That's Alex for you – damn thorough. He doesn't miss a thing. So, when he was being interviewed, he was armed with every fact about the penalties awarded to Manchester United in all his years of management. In his interview he told everyone that he thought my comments were utter rubbish and that Manchester United had had so many penalties in his time and it was no more than average, and it was ridiculous for me to suggest otherwise.

'Of course, I was unable to answer back so it was pretty frustrating for me.' Normally anyone who crosses Ferguson will receive a personal blast from the dogmatic United boss. Not Andy. He rang Ferguson the next day.

He recalls: 'Yes, we spoke the following Monday. I rang him and left a message that I wanted to speak with him, and he rang me back. I know what he's like so I wanted to clear the air. He said to me, "Listen, Andy, I'm passionate about the game, and you're passionate about football, and when two passionate people are involved there are bound to be disagreements."

'That was the end of the matter – what had to be said was said, and there was no animosity. Unfortunately, in a newspaper article I made my comments about this incident, and the headline-writer, all credit to him, put up a headline that had nothing to do with my observations. Ferguson was none too pleased and we had a row in the tunnel at Chelsea the next time he saw me.

'He had taken great exception to the headline and had a pop at me in the tunnel and I had a pop back. But the next time we met he was as right as rain. We acknowledge each other and pass a few pleasantries. We might not be bosom buddies but I have a healthy respect for him and I am sure he has a healthy respect for what I try to do.'

Gray's analysis of Ferguson's managerial career is a testimony to that healthy respect. He says: 'I can say nothing finer about Alex Ferguson than that he is probably the greatest manager in English football since Bill Shankly – and that is saying something. What he has achieved at Manchester United is phenomenal. People talk about all the wealth at the club but I don't think that is what is really important. On the playing side, in terms of success, he is on par with Shanks, who took Liverpool from the second division to the supremacy of the English game.

'If he wins the European Cup and continues to win titles for the next three to five years then we will all have to hold our hands up and say this guy is the best of them all.

'There is an argument to say that he is the tops if he wins the European Cup and then he will retire, but I would be amazed if that happens. Of course, it all depends on him but if he did land the

European Cup at last I feel he would want to go on. The adrenalin would be huge and the only thing I would worry about would be that if he did go, there would be a massive void in his life if he gave it all up.

'It was the killing of "Shanks". He died once he stopped being a manager at Liverpool. There was nothing to fill that void.

'While Alex is physically fit and still mentally alert, I think he will go on for a few more years yet. I believe that he thinks there is still work for him to do – maybe even build another side. I would just be amazed if he packed it in.'

Neil Harman

Sunday Telegraph. *Ex*-Daily Mail *chief soccer writer.*

Neil Harman was the highly respected former *Daily Mail* football correspondent who, after two major falling-outs with Alex Ferguson, will treasure the man's warm-hearted telephone call the morning after his unsavoury departure from his job. Neil says: 'Alex Ferguson and I, it would be fair to say, have had our differences. In fact, we have had two major fall-outs during my journalistic career.

'The first happened after I had written one or two things that he didn't approve of, and after winning the championship for the first time a lunch was arranged at the Royal Lancaster Hotel by the senior soccer writers in his honour – a small, intimate, off-the-record lunch which he refused to go to if I attended!

'He relented and it was during the lunch that we repaired our relationship when we were the last two sitting there and we ordered another carafe of red. By the time we'd finished it off we were strolling out of the Royal Lancaster, arms around each other's shoulders, with Alex on his way to the tube station. It was a great making-up. He is one of these guys that if you do fall out with him he will accept it if it was your honest opinion.

'However, the next time he certainly did not accept my honest opinion of the way I felt Roy Keane had behaved in the cup semi-final when he stamped on Gareth Southgate. I had written that I felt that Manchester United had taken their eye off the ball because Ferguson had been happy, so it seemed, to let Keane get away with it without rebuking him in public at least. I wrote that Manchester United were more interested in profits than morals. Alex went ballistic.

'The next day at Leicester I was confronted by an angry trio of Martin

Edwards, Sir Roland Smith and Danny McGregor in the Filbert Street press room. After the match Ferguson sneered at me during the press conference. How dare you say that Manchester United showed more interest in money than the image of their team? was the gist of their argument, while I said I was entitled to my point of view.

'For the best part of a year all I got from Ferguson was a sneer whenever he saw me. Whether on foreign trips, at the airport, boarding the plane, at games at Old Trafford or on away grounds, it was just a sneer. Then I got a little lost one day and was the last one to board a flight from Manchester with the United team. They called my name on the tannoy and it was reported back to me that Ferguson said, "Fucking leave him behind!"

'Having said that, we managed to kiss and make up again and the day after I left the *Daily Mail* in circumstances very disheartening for me I got a phone call the very next morning at 8.30 from Alex Ferguson. He told me it was the bravest thing he had ever heard of in journalism, putting my reputation before the job. He said he was sure that I would find something else and if I ever needed his help he would always be on the end of the phone for me. After 16 years I needed something like that to help me through.

'Alex Ferguson is an absolute star. A terrific guy. We may have had our fall-outs, but I've lived through them and found him to be someone who would come to your aid when you needed him the most. He is also a great manager.'

Jimmy Hill

BBC TV pundit. Former Fulham player and Coventry City manager and chairman.

Alex Ferguson called Jimmy Hill a 'prat'. The BBC television analyst had condemned Eric Cantona for a vicious tackle on Norwich City's John Polston and Ferguson took enormous exception to Hill's comments.

The outspoken champion of numerous issues has no regrets about making his stand against the challenge which he felt threatened the career of a fellow professional. The often controversial Hill makes detailed references to this incident in his book *The Jimmy Hill Story*.

Jimmy declined an invitation from Granada to appear on a TV documentary about the life and times of Ferguson for a variety of reasons, but stressed that none of them had anything to do with this personal abusive description which naturally he finds difficult to come to terms with.

Jimmy commented: 'I say in my book that after the match Alex threw a wobbly and called me a prat after I described Cantona's tackle as wild and reckless, putting John Polston's future at risk.'

Hill and Ferguson have never discussed the issue since. Hill told me: 'It's weird, we haven't met since and I suppose there has been no reason why we should. I do my work for the BBC in the studio and don't go to the grounds. I've been chairman of Fulham for the past ten years and in all that time we've never been drawn against Manchester United. I have seen him on occasions but never to chat to, and the circumstances have never arisen for that to have happened.'

So what would they say to each other if they did meet in the sort of environment where they would talk? 'We would probably have a giggle about it.' However, there is no doubt that Hill was hurt by the very nature of the word used by Ferguson. In his book, which Jimmy has painstakingly written without the help of the usual ghost writer for an autobiography, he admits to feeling 'shock and horror' by being described as a 'prat'.

Jimmy told me: 'I have said in my book that I would never hesitate to condemn any tackle that might affect a player's livelihood, and I felt that this tackle did just that. It all happened a long time ago but it's an easy line for people to write about or even remember ... oh, yes, Jimmy Hill's a prat, and it's something the fans can easily latch on to.'

They have only really met for a long chat once a long time ago, and even after that brief association Hill formed the opinion that Ferguson would be a successful manager, so much so that when he had a rocky spell at Old Trafford and his job was on the line Hill was confident he would come through it.

Hill says: 'At first Alex was never able to achieve any consistency at Manchester United and then the tongues began wagging. At that time I used to phone Martin Edwards from time to time. I am not suggesting that Martin faltered at all, but I emphasised my strong conviction that he would turn things around. It sounds silly that I should have had such faith, based on a three-hour acquaintance over half a bottle of Scotch, but nevertheless it is true. Consequently I rejoiced when he eventually did turn it around and things came good for Manchester United. He went on to become highly successful in such a short space of time that it defies belief.

'We all know that Alex has a temperamental, even tempestuous side to his character, and I don't think I mind that, so long as it is with other people – not someone who has been in his top ten supporters club!'

Hill does not subscribe to the general view that Ferguson is the best in the business when it comes to management. He puts aside all his personal feelings to make as objective an assessment as he can on whether Ferguson is the best.

'It is not really a question that can be answered. Someone like the manager of Port Vale has been a spectacular success in the light of the resources he has had and the pro rata kind of expectancy levels. It is much easier to achieve the kind of success that puts you in line to be the all-time best only if you are manager of one of the top half a dozen or so clubs in the Premiership. In my case I had five and a half years of total success in management, but no one rates me as one of the all-time best managers, and that has a lot to do with the club I managed and the fact success didn't amount to winning the first division because no one really expected that was obtainable for that kind of club ... you can't win the championship in the third division! Alex Ferguson has done as well as I expected him to do from our very first and only meeting all those years ago in Glasgow. In fact, he's done even better.'

Hill is a committed admirer of Ferguson nonetheless. He says: 'I am so pleased that the basis of his teams are English or at least British. He has used foreign players but only used them sparingly. For every foreign player he has imported he has brought on three potential candidates through the Manchester United ranks.'

David Lacey

Chief football writer, the Guardian.

The most senior soccer correspondent in the daily press has followed Fergie's fortunes, but on a personal level he says: 'I've never had a row with him – I must be a rarity!'

The award-winning, highly experienced, knowledgeable, authoritive, and amusing *Guardian* writer is a confirmed Fergie admirer.

'The most important thing – he was given time when he took over as manager. When he arrived at Old Trafford the club had not won the League for 19 years. Under Ron Atkinson they had won the cups and once or twice promised to win the League, without delivering.

'It took Ferguson seven years to win the League, yet there was a point when nobody thought he would have any better luck than Ron Atkinson in winning the title. But the club stuck with Ferguson, and that is a lesson for other big clubs – to show a bit of patience when everyone seems to demand instant success.'

Lacey pinpoints the reasons behind Ferguson's success at Old Trafford. 'He made some very important signings. Gary Pallister was crucial and, if you remember, at the time there was a great deal of discussion about paying £2 million for a defender. But now that figure looks a snip. People are now wondering about the economies of paying £10 million for Jaap Stam with the same sort of argument – "Why pay so much for a defender?" But the value of Pallister over the years has repaid that fee several times over. There have been other vital captures, such as Peter Schmeichel for under a million and, of course, Eric Cantona at a very reasonable price, and I don't think they would have won the League without those players, particularly Cantona.

'Ferguson has also stuck to a playing strategy that worked so well for him at Aberdeen. It is based on tight, efficient defence, nothing rigid such as man for man marking but a defensive base for quick and effective counterattacks. Ryan Giggs and Roy Keane were fundamental to that strategy and it is now based on Beckham, Scholes and Butt.

'Unfortunately, Ferguson has yet to win the ultimate prize in Europe. He has won the European Cup Winners' Cup, but not until he wins the Champions' League can he cross the threshold to join the likes of Bob Paisley, Jock Stein and, indeed, Sir Matt Busby. The problems are getting worse, not better, for him as the Champions' League grows. With the second-placed clubs taking part, it is increasingly more difficult to maintain momentum in the English League and make sure you are in the main event each season, while trying to win the European Cup.

'You reach a point, and that has arrived, where you have got to decide whether you really want to become a big club in terms of spending power to join the likes of Real Madrid, Barcelona and the top Italians. It might mean mortgaging yourself to have the financial power. Yet Manchester United are not exactly poor, but they have to release huge sums to bring the best in the world to Old Trafford to challenge for the Champions' League, not just this season coming up but the next as well. The club have reached that crossroads.

'Manchester United, financially, are one of the biggest clubs in the world, but on the field they are still a bit short in buying the really big names. They have to address that, otherwise they will continue winning things on a regular basis in England but the big prize in Europe might continue to elude them. They might have won it last season, or at least got to the final, but they still cannot absorb a bout of injuries or can always go out to an odd referee's decision. Eventually they will reach the final.'

Lacey wonders how long Ferguson will carry on. 'A couple of seasons ago he was talking about retirement but now he seems to have got his second wind.'

Denis Law

Manchester United legend. Radio analyst.

Few people in the game are equipped to compare Alex Ferguson with Sir Matt Busby. The Law man is one of the few. The Scottish international goalscoring phenomenon played in Sir Matt's European Cup-winning team as part of that legendary trio – Law, Charlton, Best – and he has been one of Ferguson's long-standing friends.

Law says: 'Yes, I have known Alex for a long, long time, going back to the '60s when he was still playing in Scotland. I thought then that here was a guy who craved success and would get what he wanted because he knew what he wanted to achieve in life.

'Celtic and Rangers dominated Scottish football then as they do now and yet he took Aberdeen to the very top, and that in itself – bearing in mind the strength of both Celtic and Rangers – was a great achievement and gave you the feeling he could do it elsewhere. He took Aberdeen to the championship and triumphs in Europe, including winning the Cup Winners' Cup, but coming down to England is always a difficult job and he did have a couple of years when it didn't go particularly well for him but then everything slotted into place.

'His achievements have been truly fantastic. He has been slightly unfortunate not to win the European Cup – I still call it the European Cup as I cannot bring myself to describe it as the Champions' League. I thought he would win it a couple of years ago but they were beaten in the semi-final by Borussia Dortmund. Then I was convinced that with that amount of experience in their team they would definitely win it the following year, but they just seemed to run out of steam.

'Certainly I would put Alex right up there alongside the great managers of all time, like "Shanks", Busby and Jock Stein, particularly for what Jock achieved in Scottish football as well. Alex has been very much like Sir Matt in the way that he has brought the youth through at Old Trafford. Not only have they emerged in the United first team, they have become permanent fixtures. Not only that, they have progressed to the international team and become a permanent fixture there, too. With Alex's experience in the transfer market in buying the right players, coupled with the youth structure that has become a formidable combination, really, you can't do much better than that.

'Alex has great stature in the game and quite rightly so, and it is important that he has also chosen the right back-room staff, very much in the style of Sir Matt, "Shanks" and Jock Stein. Behind the scenes he has got everyone rooting for the club. He has built a family atmosphere and you need that to pull through defeats and cope with the pressures.

'I agree that Alex needs to win the European Cup to be considered as the very best. He has qualified for another crack at it, and I feel there is still a great possibility that he can do it finally this time. There wasn't the same pressure as going in as champions again, and I am sure they will have learned by their previous experiences. It was disappointing, losing the championship, but the consolation is that they finished runners-up to qualify for the European Cup again.'

Denis has a sound personal relationship with Alex – they haven't even had a disagreement in all the years they've known each other. Law knows about his volatile reputation but he has not experienced it at first hand. 'Alex can be under a great deal of pressure and sometimes you cannot blame him for the way he feels. He is under scrutiny all the time and it must get to him at times. He is a different character to Sir Matt, and we've all heard that he can be a touch abrasive, but there were times when Sir Matt could blow a bit, although not as often as Alex!'

Mark Lawrenson

BBC Match of the Day, Football Focus.

Mark Lawrenson has earned a reputation for being a forthright, no-nonsense TV pundit. So, as you'd expect, the former Liverpool star and Oxford manager doesn't mince his words when it comes to an assessment of Alex Ferguson.

'He's ruthless.'

However, Lawrenson doesn't feel this is detrimental in a soccer manager – in fact, he is paying Fergie a huge compliment. He explained: 'Even managers like genial Bob Paisley had a ruthless streak, and Fergie certainly has it. I don't know if that's a northern trait, but it's certainly something that the northern managers seem to possess.

'Alex Ferguson was a relative failure at Old Trafford in his first few years, but there is something that drives him on from inside that ensured he wasn't going to go out a failure. Having said that, he owes a big thank-you to the Manchester United board because they could easily have lost patience and said, "Thanks very much, but no thanks." Instead, they kept faith in him and Alex went on to prove what a great manager he is.

'He's a winner. Nothing else interests him. The great acid test is that all the top players want to play for him.'

Ferguson doesn't accept criticism with good grace. He hates it. Lawrenson says: 'We get on very well. Yet I have been critical of him and his team in the past as far as failure in Europe is concerned, and for Fergie and the club that is the Big One. If he has objected, he has never said anything to me about it.

'But I always believe in what I have to say and I have suggested that he is still one rung away from the likes of Paisley and Shankly and, indeed, Sir Matt until he wins the Champions' League. He has got to win the ultimate prize before he can be regarded in that category. It's not easy for him because the format has changed and that has made the competition harder to win. To win the Champions' League, I am sure, is what drives him on.'

Mark had plenty to say about Manchester United's Champions' League exit last season in his *Mirror* column. He wrote: 'While watching Juventus systematically destroy Monaco, I *couldn't* help thinking about Manchester United. They are the best team this country has to offer, yet they went out of the European Cup at the quarter-final stage. They would certainly be one of the eight teams in Europe, but the top spots are still exclusively reserved for certain sides. Look at the facts: Manchester United failed to beat Monaco over two legs – hell, they even failed to score against them over two legs. And what about Juventus? They ripped Monaco apart. So I hope that maybe people will realise that, much as our game has improved, English clubs are still streets behind the best. Look at the facts: Juve were beaten 3–2 by United at Old Trafford in October. It was a fantastic display by Fergie's boys and they thoroughly deserved to win. That, allied to the goalless draw against Italy in Rome earlier in the month, suddenly had people proclaiming that we were the best in the world again. But all evidence since then has pointed to the contrary. United beat Juventus when they were in the form of their lives, while the Italians were struggling domestically. They had a wonderful chance to put a depleted Juve out of the competition in Turin, but Marcello Lippi's boys scraped in.'

Des Lynam

BBC Match of the Day. *Top sports presenter.*

Laid-back. Yes. Not quite as far laid-back as Ruud Gullit, but certainly the most relaxed sports presenter of his generation. The style is languid, totally professional and most definitely charismatic. His studio techniques are perfectly designed to pose the questions for the more direct, even ruthless, abrasive pundits to put over their more controversial points of view. Hardly the sort of chap who would rub anyone the wrong way.

Then, of course, there's always Alex Ferguson.

Genial Des made a chance comment that seemed to upset Fergie far more than he imagined. Des takes up the tale of misunderstanding. 'Alex did take me to task for supposedly telling him how to run his football club – as if I would try to do that. Let's face it, no one would dare to tell Alex Ferguson how to run his football club. Certainly not me.

'It was no more than a chance remark about the development of the young players at Manchester United at about the time that Ryan Giggs was still a teenager. I posed a question to Alan Hansen on TV something like, "Alex Ferguson does a marvellous job at Old Trafford, particularly protecting these young men from people like us. I wonder if it's time to take the gag off and allow a player like Ryan Giggs to talk to the media?" Alan Hansen's response was, I recall, brief but to the point and he suggested that Alex should indeed let the players off the leash.

'For some reason Alex interpreted that as telling him how to run his club. He certainly had a bee in his bonnet about it because a little later on in his video he responded to what I had said. It seemed to me that he had briefed the interviewer to ask him the question about my remark on *Match of the Day*. Alex responded, "He's been trying to tell me how I should run my football club."

'I was slightly amazed by it all, if not disturbed, to be truthful. I have spent my entire life in television without trying to put myself forward as some sort of expert, so it was very bizarre to say the least. I can only assume that Alex had got the wrong end of the stick and perhaps hadn't actually seen or heard what had occurred but had been told by someone.

'A couple of years ago I conducted a face-to-face interview before the FA Cup Final and we spent a very pleasant time together, discussing the football issues over a glass or two of champagne. The subject of his displeasure was not raised. Had it been, I would have simply told him precisely what I've told you...'

In reality, Des and Alex have no problems on a personal level. Des says: 'We get on just fine. We are much the same sort of age. I'm 55, a year younger than Alex, but we're of the same generation. I have a great regard for him. I have nothing but admiration for those who are not given the greatest hand of cards when they start out in life but deal with the cards they've got magnificently.'

Ferguson's schizophrenia is hardly a soccer secret. Des says: 'I admire his ability as a football manager. He has undoubtedly proved himself the best in the business in recent years in this country. I sometimes find his public image comes across a little harsh and that is probably the reason why some people don't like him.

'Personally, I admire Alex for being himself rather than trying to be cosmetic, particularly in front of the cameras. Many people act out a role on TV and are something quite different off-screen. He doesn't bother. Alex has the courage of his convictions to be himself even on camera.

'He doesn't suffer fools and nor is he prepared to be overtly friendly toward the media or try to gain any special treatment from us.

'Direct. That's the best way to describe his attitude. I would certainly say that. It's a brave man who would tell Alex Ferguson how to conduct himself or to run his team. Sometimes it has to be done. But it hasn't been done by me!'

David Meek

Football writer, Manchester Evening News, *for more than 40 years. Now retired.*

David Meek, who is now in charge of the Manchester United press box, reckons that Alex Ferguson is the best of the *seven* managers he has been associated with. Meek, who worked with Sir Matt Busby, a great publicist, says that Ferguson gets the accolade because he was 'like a breath of fresh air' when he took over at Old Trafford.

Meek, as an *Evening* newspaper man, relished the fact that Ferguson was always sitting at his desk at the training ground every morning at the crack of dawn. 'He was the *Evening* newspaper man's dream,' said Meek. 'He always kept me in the picture in time for the first edition. Having worked with a previous United manager who used to turn up for training at about 10.30 a.m. and would say, "Nothing has happened yet today," Ferguson showed he knew what it was all about. You can't ask for any more than that. He was always there when you needed him and always available and co-operative.'

John Motson

BBC commentator.

John Motson has been on the receiving end of the Jekyll and Hyde character of Alex Ferguson. When Fergie is in the mood there are few managers in the game more accommodating or helpful, as Motson discovered in his first dealings with him at Aberdeen. As you would expect from the stickler for statistics, John remembers the precise match!

Motson recalls: 'I remember when I was covering Aberdeen versus Liverpool in the European Cup in 1980. I had never met Alex before but I phoned him up and told him I was doing the commentary for the English viewers and requested his help about his players. He made a special journey out to my hotel to help me out with the background on the club and his team. I thought then that he was a man going places with a sense for public relations.'

Ferguson recognised the power of the media, but hasn't always been such a diplomat. Yet Motson has not found Ferguson to be a man who holds a grudge. Motson continued: 'When he joined Manchester United I had a lot of dealings with him, and I must say I have had a slight fall-out on a couple of interviews. Once I asked him a couple of questions immediately after a match that were near the mark for him. He got just a little bit cross! But the next time I bumped into him, all had been forgotten.'

Memory man Motson couldn't remember the particulars of the after-match interview row, although it might well have been the occasion of a Roy Keane sending off when Ferguson was more than a touch touchy. Whatever the details of the momentary falling-out, Motson retains nothing but admiration for Ferguson. 'Of all the managers he seems to be the one who is at his desk the earliest in the mornings. If you ring him at 8.30 a.m. you know he'll be there at his training-ground office.'

As for Ferguson's record, Motson adds: 'How many men have won seven championships? Very few, apart from Jock Stein and Walter Smith whose achievements were all in Scotland. In modern times no one has won more championships on both sides of the border.

'What I admire most about him is that in an era when player power has taken over in a lot of places, he has remained one of the few strict managers in the mould of Brian Clough and Bill Shankly. Let's face it, that isn't so easy these days when the players are paid so much and can be millionaires before the age of 21.

'I've also seen the other side of Alex, a hugely compassionate guy. He lost one of his real big mates in Scotland about a year ago and he was really cut up about it. I'm sure it's his competitive edge that puts people's backs up because his attitude is all about winning, but there is a kind side to him that I've discovered because of my family problem. Every time I met him he would ask about Ann's health. 'I'd be saying a prayer for her,' he would say to me.

'That's all the more incredible considering that on one occasion he had some very strong words. However, Alex might give you a bollocking but the next time he sees you he doesn't ignore you. You can take his bollocking on the chin or finish up disliking him for the rest of your life.

'I was presenting *Football Focus* and Liam Brady made some observations at the time when Alex was really struggling and under pressure at Manchester United and there was even discussion about his position and whether his job was on the line. Liam's comments centred around the defensive organisation of the team and the tactics which he said the purists would not approve of, remembering the Busby Babes and how they played.

'The next day I just happened to be going to see Ferguson, and as I collect signatures in books I took one of his books with me to Highbury ... He didn't sign it. Instead, he gave me a piece of his mind. I found it hard to take as the comments had been made by someone else, but Alex felt that I shouldn't have allowed Liam Brady to have made his remarks. He had a real attack about what Liam had said the previous day.'

Dennis Signy

Doyen of football writers. Written for national papers from The Times *to the* News of the World. *One-time general manager of Brentford and chief executive of QPR. Currently PR consultant to the Football League.*

Dennis Signy, OBE, former editor of the *Hendon Times* and close friend of Margaret Thatcher, met Ferguson in the dressing room on his first day in charge at Old Trafford. Signy, who was attached to QPR at the time, said: 'From that day to this Ferguson has been a friend to me and is completely different to his public persona. He is charming – he carried my wife Pats' bags to her car after a function in London – and humorous. He is a family man who can switch off from football when the occasion demands.

'As a football manager he ranks among the top of the greats I have met in my 50 years in football. His success at Manchester United speaks for itself.

'He has always been co-operative and has been conscious that the image of United is correctly projected. When Eric Cantona was controversially chosen by the FWA as the Footballer of the Year, I rang Alex and expressed concern that Cantona might not turn up because of the adverse publicity he had received after the Crystal Palace incident. Alex replied: "He'll be there". Enlisting the help of his secretary he organised a car from Manchester to the Royal Lancaster hotel in London and travelled down with him.'

Tom Tyrell

Former Piccadilly Radio football commentator.

The day Alex Ferguson walked through the doors of Old Trafford one of his first tasks was to acquaint himself with the local media. Tom's relationship with him goes back to Ferguson's first day at the club as the new manager, and he has dealt with Fergie virtually on a daily basis ever since.

Tom has been covering Manchester United for local radio since 1970 and locally for 31 years in total. 'I interviewed Alex Ferguson on the morning he arrived at the club, the first radio interview he did, and I have interviewed him ever since on a regular basis. His record speaks for itself. If he wins one more championship he will equal Sir Matt's record of five in 1952, '56, '57, '65 and '67. He has already won the FA Cup more times than Sir Matt.

'In my opinion, Alex is the best ever Manchester United manager. Sir Matt is The Boss – he was such a loving sort of person, while Alex is a totally different character, but even so he treats me like his nephew and has always been very, very good to me over the years, although he never gives you any clues about his transfer targets.

'I once said to him that Manchester United ought to try to be like Southampton in the way that they signed Kevin Keegan without anyone knowing and they just unveiled him at a press conference when they whipped back the curtain and there he was. I think he liked that idea. But I do feel the club's public relations could be much better, and their relationship with the media could improve if they had somebody from the media taking on that task.'

Ferguson, however, has little time for his public image. He wants success and more trophies and that is the image he wishes to convey.

Tom says: 'If he were to win the European Cup or one more championship there can be no doubt that he would be Manchester United's most successful manager and, indeed, the most successful manager in British football.'

Tom knows Ferguson as well as anyone in the media. He says: 'A lot of people don't know the side of Alex where he has such a tremendous sense of humour. He can be a practical joker as well. I asked him to join in one of my jokes on 1 April. At the time there was a huge debate about the merits of artificial surfaces – it must have been back in 1987 – and at the same time the club were having enormous problems with the Old Trafford playing surface. I came up with this practical joke about how Manchester United were to resolve their problems with the pitch with a revolutionary plastic one.

'I conducted a mock interview with Alex where we both ended up in fits of laughter which I had to later edit out. He took it a stage further and said on air that Manchester United would be installing a synthetic pitch and it would be a red one! He said that the plastic pitch had been perfected by Swedish scientists and that the "grass" was the closest to the real thing. Alex also said they would have illuminated goalposts, which would flash whenever anyone scored!

'On the air we actually had an interview with a Swedish scientist, talking about the synthetic surface. That night on BBC North, the regional TV programme, they showed a picture of Old Trafford with the playing surface red!

'It was the best April Fool's joke we have ever pulled off – it was a real cracker. Whenever I think of an April Fool's joke, I think of that one.'

There was more from the Ferguson Book of Jokes. Tom recalls: 'He got me to interview a young Manchester United player and he wanted me to be particularly hard on him for some reason. He wanted me to put the poor kid on the spot, and to ask him pre-arranged questions while Alex and his assistant Brian Kidd were hiding in a position where they could hear the boy's answers. I really put the lad through it, trying to keep a straight face.'

Tom was the victim of a Ferguson practical joke when he asked the manager's permission to interview Ryan Giggs after he'd taken part in the United team which had won the Youth Cup final of 1992 but had just lost the championship to Leeds after losing at Liverpool. I stood in the corridor with my microphone in my hand but I hooked it under my strap. Alex had agreed that I could do the first interview with Ryan

Giggs. George Switzer, who played in the Youth final at full back, one of the boys who didn't make it, came down the corridor and stood beside me in his shirt, shorts and socks, and was on tiptoe talking into the microphone. 'I said, "all right, George, it was quite a good game." He said, "Yeah, it was a fantastic game."

'I suddenly realised what was going on.

'Fergie and Kidd were like the Marx brothers with their heads popping round the corner with Eric Harrison joining them. I had asked to interview Ryan Giggs, but they had sent out George instead.'

But it's not all been laughing and joking with Ferguson. Far from it. 'I've faced his wrath on a few occasions,' said Tom, 'but each time I felt I was the innocent party.

'Although he will blast off at you, the next day you can be best friends again. It's usually a case of a misunderstanding as far as I'm concerned.

'The first time, he accused me of always being at the club. I was there doing a phone-in programme. But I was always at the club, and he knew it, and had never objected before so I couldn't quite understand that blast. I put it down to a "bad hair day". I was the one around the place and he picked on me.

'Tommy Docherty has been an outspoken critic of the team, of Ferguson, particularly in the early stages of his management, and had written something that Alex clearly didn't like in a newspaper article. At the same time he was working for us at Piccadilly Radio. It reached the stage where the players refused to speak to us and Ferguson made reference to this in the press room where everybody heard it. A couple of the national papers picked it up, asked me about it and it appeared in the press the next day. I was asked, "You would think Manchester United was bigger than this, wouldn't you?" I replied, "Yes." Unfortunately it turned out that I was quoted as saying, "Manchester United should be bigger than this."

'When you fall out with Ferguson you have to sample "the Hairdryer". It was coined by Gordon Strachan. Alex Ferguson puts his face right up to yours and shouts – it feels like a blast from a hairdryer!

'I was on the receiving end of the Hairdryer on another occasion when there was yet another total misunderstanding. Eddie Booth used to work in the Old Trafford press box for the best part of a generation, a lovely old guy who I used to help out on occasions. I put out a story for the Press Association on one of those times I was helping out Eddie. It concerned Ferguson's complaints about the Christmas fixtures last year when Manchester United had to play at Chelsea with a noon kick-off on Boxing Day and then away to Southampton on New Year's Eve. Ferguson had said that they hadn't really considered the fans, although it didn't really matter to the players and to himself because they were used to being away over Christmas and New Year.

'He was more concerned about people like myself who had to drive all the way to London early in the morning for the early kick-off on Boxing Day and then drive to Southampton and back on New Year's Eve. The story was given a twist by the newspapers that Alex clearly didn't approve of and blamed me for it. It was reported that a whinging Ferguson wanted to cancel Christmas football.

'When he caught sight of me at Stamford Bridge he let rip. This was the only time when someone saw him having a go at me. I said to Alex that it would be better if we sorted it out outside. It must have sounded as if we were going to have a fight, which, of course, was not the case. The next day he invited me into his office, we had a cup of tea and sorted out our differences.

'It's never pleasant, having a row with anyone, but one of his strengths is that he doesn't do anything devious because he has fallen out with you. It's always up front and instantaneous, shouting and screaming, but then it's finished.

'I've always been a United fan and held the United manager, whoever he is, in high esteem. I've got to know them over the years, and you find out they are only human after all, with their own peculiar frailties and nuances. In fact, they are really like everybody else. I have always got on with Alex, and it's been no problem.'

Tom recalls many a conversation with Strachan about the manager's cup-throwing storms inside the dressing room, and he has witnessed others on the receiving end of the bad hair day when the Hairdryer goes to work.

Bob Wilson

ITV's main football presenter. Arsenal's goalkeeping coach.

Bob Wilson is one of the most respected individuals in the game. Born in Chesterfield, he was part of the Arsenal Double side in 1971, and became the first English-born player to be capped for Scotland – after representing England Schoolboys in 1957. He is still active inside the game, coaching David Seaman at Highbury.

He says: 'Appreciation of Alex Ferguson's talents come down to his will to win; I've never met someone with such passion to be a winner. I would talk about Alex in the same breath as Bill Shankly and Jock Stein – that's all I can do. I got to know Shanks and he was the greatest character I have ever met. Jock Stein once gave me a bollocking but that's another story. Shanks was a great psychologist and Alex has a lot of that, too. I remember the day before the FA Cup Final. It was piddling down and when he saw me he said, "Aye, Bob, have a good game tomorrow ... but the pitch will be a nightmare for goalkeepers." Jock Stein had presence. Both of them were also winners, but I'm not sure they had bigger determination to win than Alex.'